E3-95
LR20038

N

TIE-DYED PAPER

Anne Maile

TIE-DYED PAPER

Mills & Boon Limited,
London

First published in Great Britain 1975 by Mills &
Boon Limited, 17–19 Foley Street, London W1A
1DR.

ISBN 0 263 05610 4

Printed in Great Britain by
J. W. Arrowsmith Ltd.
Winterstoke Road, Bristol BS3 2NT.

ACKNOWLEDGEMENTS

I would like to thank Miss M. P. Abbott, headmistress of Horniman Primary School, and members of her staff for their willing and enthusiastic co-operation in allowing me to try out tie-dyed paper experiments with their pupils. For me it was a great pleasure, and, as the results were surprisingly good, also very gratifying. Some of the children's work is shown in colour plates 31–33.

I am much indebted to Mr North, of K. B. Cameras Ltd., who has kindly helped in many ways, giving me professional advice on photographic problems.

I am most grateful to Mrs Joan Bryant of Mills & Boon Ltd, who encouraged me to develop my ideas about tie-dyed paper and to continue with the necessary work and research on the subject to produce this book. I would also like to pay tribute to Miss Barbara Horn, my editor, whose capable assistance has been invaluable.

Finally, I would like to thank my husband, whose readiness to help in all practical matters is greatly appreciated.

Dedicated to my three sons, John, Richard and Geoffrey, who are very dear to me.

CONTENTS

	Page
Introduction	9
Tie-dyed paper	11
How to tie-dye paper	12
What you need	13
Paper for tie-dyeing	15
Pegs and clips	32
Binding	36
Marbling	39
Twisting	42
Rolling	44
Wrapping paper round bases	49
Sandwiching paper between wood	54
Folding and pleating	58
Dyeing	83
Colouring matter other than dyes	85
Dyes	86
The dyeing process	88
Rinsing	95
Draining the samples	96
Straightening out and ironing	97
Storing the samples	98
Weak spots, holes and tears	99
Adhesives	100
Group work	101
Constructing simple patterns and designs	103
Making collages and murals	108
Paper weaving	111
Posters	112
Origami	113
Mobiles	115
Dolls	117
Simple hand puppets	119
Masks	120
Fancy dresses	121
Hats	123
Paper flowers	128
Making things	131
Suppliers	136

INTRODUCTION

Tie-dyed paper! An unlikely proposition one would think!

I first began to experiment with tie-dyed paper some years ago after I saw some Japanese hand-made paper that had obviously been patterned by a kind of tie-dyeing process. This set me thinking and made me impatient to try some for myself. I obtained several types of hand-made papers and tie-dyed them along with my fabrics. The results were most gratifying. Thus encouraged, a period followed in which every type of paper I could find was folded up in every possible way and immersed in dye. Small bowls, old cups, and jam jars containing leftover dye from fabric dyeing, enclosed in a cardboard box to prevent accidents, were part of my kitchen scene. This meant that odd bits of tied-up paper could be popped into dye at any spare moment during the day, with an old spoon handy to fish them out and put them on newspaper to drain.

In a very short time I had a sizeable batch of papers, some good, some not so good. After assessing the results I started again, eliminating many of the obvious mistakes. I soon had a large folio of interesting tie-dyed papers and a few collages made from odd damaged pieccs, too.

During my lectures on tie-dyeing fabric, the papers were shown as a point of interest and as a useful way of practising the folding methods – an adjunct to fabric tie-dyeing.

Several years later I became involved with young children, three to eight years old, attempting to do fabric tie-dyeing for the first time. Everything went well, but we soon used up the supply of old sheets and

Tie-dyed paper from Japan; folded with edges and corners dip-dyed

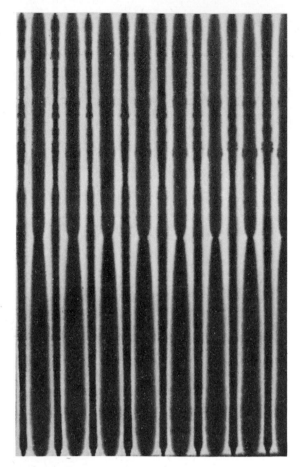

Tie-dyed paper from Japan; stripes in one colour

olds to bunch up and fold it freely, adding pegs and rubber bands to hold the bundles in place while the dyeing was done. The anticipated mishaps did not occur and the general atmosphere was of busily and happily engrossed children. Later, two colourful murals and other decorative panels were created from the tie-dyed papers. Following this, a class of younger children successfully dip-dyed some soft absorbent napkins, tissues and crêpe paper for decorations and paper flowers. Teachers from other schools carried out more experiments in tie-dyeing paper with pupils of various ages, who found it great fun to do. They all agree that the craft offers great scope for originality and that the colourful tie-dyed papers can be put to innumerable uses.

At first I was very conscious of the creases left in the samples after dyeing. Some were slight and could be ironed out, but others were more permanent. After a time I grew to accept them as part of the finished product, even emphasising some to suggest rugged textures in collages and various other projects.

cloth available, and new cloth was prohibitive in price. There *was* an alternative, and it was cheap, easy to obtain, with nothing to lose or worry about if it did not turn out successfully – PAPER. The headmistress of a local school was willing to allow her pupils to be my guinea pigs.

We collected paper of all kinds – much of it waste – and allowed a class of seven-year-

Having established that tie-dyeing paper is an interesting, cheap and practical craft for schoolchildren, the next thing to do was to develop and extend the scope of the craft to suit adults. I hope the illustrations of articles made of tie-dyed paper and the many ideas for its use given in this book will prove convincing. As far as I am concerned, tie-dyed paper has come to stay, not only as an adjunct to fabric tie-dye, but also as a craft in its own right.

A. M.

TIE-DYED PAPER

When a flat piece of paper is put in dye the entire surface becomes coloured. If a piece of paper is crumpled or folded, then tied into a bundle before being dyed, only the parts on the outside become coloured. The inside areas remain undyed. This is called resist dyeing and the undyed parts are called resist areas. The kind of pattern that eventually emerges, composed of dyed and undyed parts, can be controlled by the tying-up methods. That is why the craft is called tie-dyeing.

The terms 'tie-up' and 'tying-up' include all methods of manipulating the paper to form it into a bundle, whether or not anything on it is actually tied-up. Tied-up samples, referred to as 'bundles', can be bound with string or thread, but they are still 'tied-up' even if pegs, clips, rubber bands or any other means have been used to contain them.

HOW TO TIE-DYE PAPER

There are three stages in tie-dyeing paper.

Tying-up Form a piece of paper into a bundle by crumpling, folding, pleating or rolling. Hold it in place with pegs, clips or rubber bands, or bind it with thread or string.

Dyeing Place the bundle in dye or coloured liquid.

Drying When dry, undo the bundle very carefully.

The sample is now dyed in one colour. To dye it in more than one colour, tie up the bundle and treat it in one of the following ways.

Dye the whole bundle in the first colour. Dry, but do not undo. Then immerse one or both ends or certain parts of the bundle in the second colour. Drain, dry and undo.

Dye only parts of the sample in the first colour. Drain and dry. Dye the remaining parts in the second colour. Dry and undo.

Apply different-coloured dyes to the sample with a brush at any stage, before or after the first or second dyeing.

Tie-up and dye in the first colour. Dry and undo. Tie-up the sample again, rearranging and refolding it so that any undyed areas are brought to the outside of the bundle. Dye in the second colour. Dry and undo.

WHAT YOU NEED

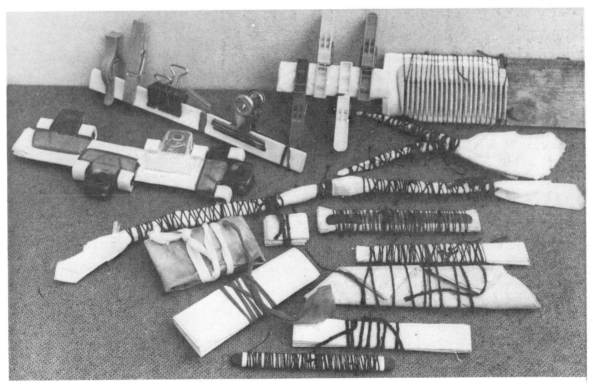

Tied-up bundles showing various methods

PAPER

All kinds and sizes, white, pastel-coloured, certain types of brown paper, even waste paper.

COLOURING MATTER

Household and liquid dyes, Dylon cold water dyes, Procion M, H and other reactive dyes, direct and basic dyes, coloured inks (ready-mixed or in powder form), powdered inks (such as Brusho), school powder colours.

DYE VESSELS

As most of the dyeing is done cold, the range of dye vessels is almost limitless. Saucepans; bowls; basins; pie dishes; all enamel, pot, glass or plastic vessels, jam jars; even empty tins or waxed cartons can be used.

ADHESIVES

All kinds of gum, glue, PVA adhesive, wallpaper paste, flour and water paste are suitable. In some cases photographic

13

mounting tissue, such as Ademco, or other bonding tissue is valuable.

FASTENINGS AND BINDINGS

Clothes pegs and clips of all types, pipe cleaners, garden ties and rubber bands give good results. For binding, use any of the following: most threads, yarns, strings, raffia, tape, and strips of torn cloth, old nylon stockings and tights.

OTHER USEFUL ITEMS

Scissors, pins, brushes for applying dye and adhesive, spoons, rubber gloves, and an iron.

Encourage the children who are going to tie-dye paper to collect newspaper, bottles, jam jars, paper bags of all colours, poly-thene bags, boxes and cartons for making models, scraps of waste paper, envelopes, typing papers clean on one side, paper used for wrapping food and clothes, lolly and ice cream sticks, and flat pieces from date boxes. Save all odd pieces of string and thread for bindings.

Useful items for tie-dyeing paper

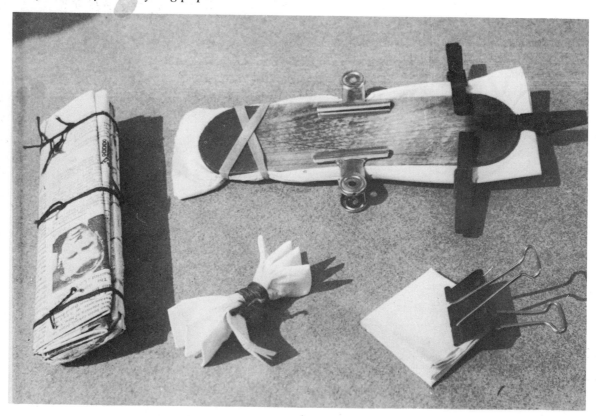

PAPER FOR TIE-DYEING

The type of paper used is an important factor in tie-dyeing. There are three main categories of paper.

SOFT AND VERY ABSORBENT PAPERS

These papers soak up the dye instantly. They are usually manufactured for the sole purpose of soaking up liquids and wiping things clean and dry, such as paper napkins, tissues, kitchen roll, paper towels, etc. They need only a short dip, as the dye spreads rapidly from the point of contact in all directions along the paper fibre. If immersed for too long, the whole sample becomes flooded with dye.

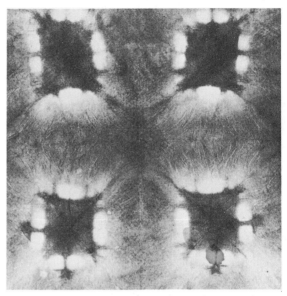

Paper napkin folded as D20, then in half, two pegs added. The points dyed a darker colour

Paper napkin folded into quarters and gathered into a bundle. Each side dyed a different colour

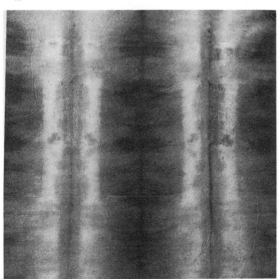

Soft papers are very good for the marbling and twisting methods, and are excellent for your first experiments with tie-dye. They provide a means of getting quick, colourful results and a chance to find out how the paper reacts to the dye. It is fun dipping different parts of the sample in various colours and watching the dyes spread and blend to produce many unexpected effects. Even three- and four-year-olds can manage simple exercises with tissues and cheap paper napkins. It does not really matter if they are bunched or folded haphazardly; accuracy in tying up is not vital at this stage. Irregular blobs of colour will be produced instead of a set design.

Two examples of dip-dyed paper napkins

wrapped around the bundle tightly enough to be effective, they are difficult to remove without nipping out a piece of the paper at the same time. To prevent this happening, insert a matchstick under one part of the rubber band before dyeing; it can be used as a lever for lifting off the rubber band afterwards.

All absorbent papers should be thoroughly dried out before you attempt to undo them. The various layers in the bundle tend to stick together while they are wet, and so holes will be caused if they are forced apart.

Newspaper and blotting paper are not recommended for tie-dyeing.

MEDIUM ABSORBENT PAPERS

These papers are stronger in texture than soft ones, and the dye takes longer to penetrate them properly.

This group, which is the most suitable for tie-dyeing, includes a very wide range of papers, some more absorbent or tougher than others. Only those that are easy to obtain are mentioned. In different localities special papers may be found that might be excellent for dyeing. Look around and test any that seem promising.

Some papers that have been well-tested and give very successful results are cartridge and shelf paper, plain white florist's paper, all kinds of typing and note papers, plain wallpaper or lining paper, newsprint, greaseproof paper, white wrapping paper used in shops for covering food and clothing, paper bags, paper tablecloths, doilies and old envelopes. The white corrugated wrappings from packets of biscuits serve many purposes. The foil wrappings with a thin layer of white paper, used for covering chocolate biscuits, give interesting luminous effects when dyed. They need no binding; crumple or fold them firmly and leave

For holding this type of sample, pegs and clips are more satisfactory than binding or rubber bands. If binding has to be used, choose soft string, raffia, or strips of torn cloth or nylon. The fine harder threads cut into the soft paper when it becomes wet, leaving holes in the sample. Rubber bands are not very successful either. If they are

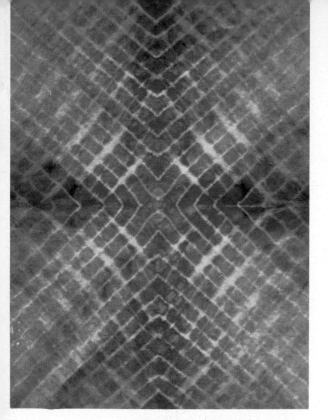

1   *Imitation Japanese paper no. 3, folded, accordion pleated, and bound*

2   *Tissue paper folded and pegs added*

3   *Tissue paper folded and bound*

4   *Tissue paper folded, bound, and corners dipped in darker dye*

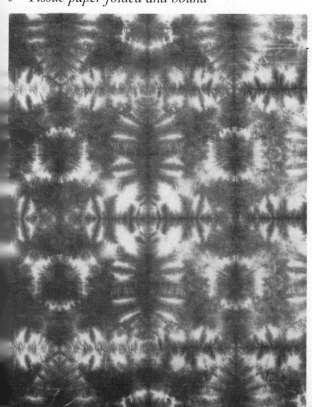

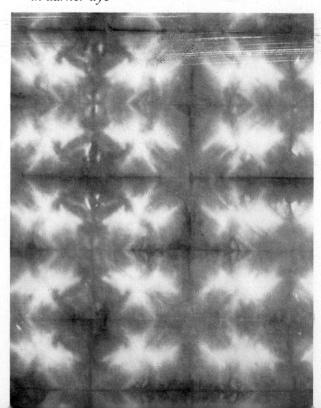

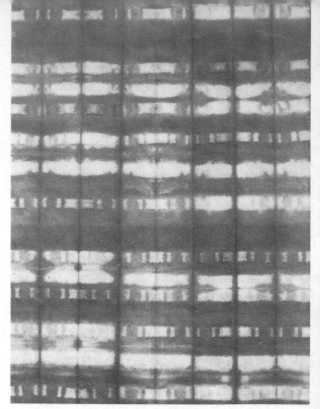

5 *Tiny squares of typing paper pivot pleated and arranged on a contrasting background*

6 *Tissue paper folded lengthways and across, with pegs added on one side*

7 *Greaseproof paper twisted, bound, and dyed twice*

8 *Squares folded in different ways*

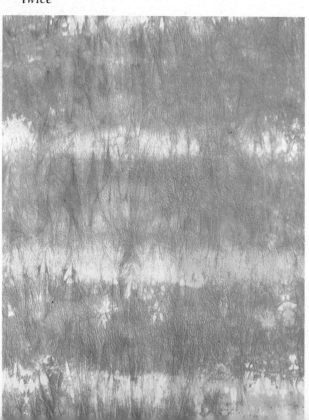

them in the dye for several hours or overnight. Medium absorbent papers can generally be adapted to most tying-up methods. The dyeing time may vary from 15 minutes to 4 hours or more, depending on the absorbency of the paper and the bulk of the bundle.

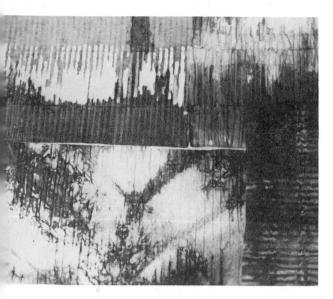

Corrugated paper used for wrapping biscuits

HARDER, LESS ABSORBENT PAPERS

Some of these papers are tough or thick, and have only a limited use in tie-dyeing. Cellophane, polythene, tracing paper and waxed paper cannot be tie-dyed. Some shiny papers will only absorb a little of the dye, remaining pale in colour.

There are others, such as white and brown packing paper, special surfaced papers, some wallpapers, etc., that are worth persevering with because of their extra strength and size. They will respond if treated in one or more of the following ways.

(*a*) Leave the sample in the dye for 12–24

hours. It will be obvious when the sample has accepted the dye properly.

(*b*) Dye small sections at a time, undoing, refolding and rearranging the sample each time so that different areas become patterned.

(*c*) Hot dyeing gives better penetration than cold dyeing. Dye until the paper absorbs the colour.

(*d*) Make the paper more pliable, and thus more receptive to the dye, by gently 'scrubbing' and crumpling it in the palms of the hands before folding.

(*e*) Soak the folded, but not bound, sample in hot or cold water before dyeing (see greaseproof paper, pages 22–24).

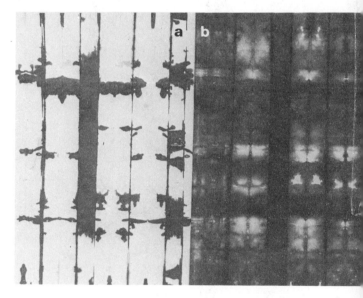

Thick hard paper: (a) effect after normal tying up and dyeing, (b) effect when sample is crumpled first, then tied up with looser and less binding and soaked in hot water for thirty minutes before dyeing

COLOURED PAPERS

You need not be restricted to white paper. However, the background colour of the paper influences the colour dyed over it.

17

Only pure white paper produces a clean-looking version of the true colour of the dye. Cream and pastel papers add variety to many projects, but any colours dyed on them are duller. Dyes of contrasting colour to the paper itself are particularly affected in this way. Strong colours are best for tinted papers, otherwise the pattern will be rather indefinite.

ESPECIALLY GOOD PAPERS FOR TIE-DYEING

There are certain easily-obtainable papers particularly useful for many tie-dye projects that need special handling to get the best results. These are listed under separate headings for easy reference. If you follow the information and suggestions, you should avoid initial disappointments.

TISSUE PAPER

This can be bought in sheets, approximately 50 × 75cm (20″ × 30″). Quite often the less expensive, coarser type is better for tie-dyeing. Although an absorbent paper, the firm texture prevents the dye from spreading outwards quite as rapidly as in softer papers.

Tissue paper is neither tough nor strong, especially when wet. This fact must be accepted and allowed for. Even with gentle handling, expect to make some tears and holes in your first samples. But *do not* throw these away. You will find innumerable uses for quite badly torn samples when you make collages and other things with your tie-dyed papers.

Tissue paper is so pliable that with careful treatment almost any tying-up method can be carried out. Begin with simple folding methods (see pages 58–62), using pegs and clips to hold the bundle in place. For your first binding experiments use soft string, yarns, raffia, strips of torn cloth or nylon stocking, which do not cut into the paper

when it is wet. Bind without exerting too much tension on the sample.

To create a definite resist area you must make a solid band of taut binding without damaging the fragile paper. To do this, first pleat or squeeze in the sample to form a narrow 'waist'. Then add tight binding at least 1·5cm ($\frac{1}{2}$″) wide or the dye will seep underneath. A strip of polythene can be wrapped round the sample before applying the binding.

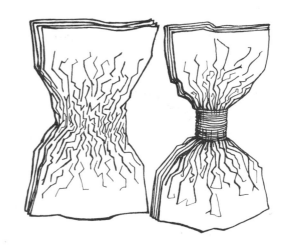

Tissue paper folded in half lengthways, then crushed into a waist before binding

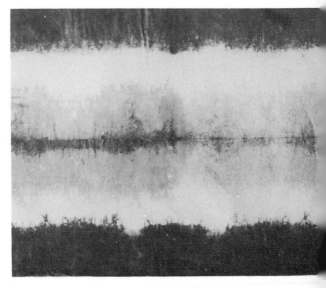

When working with very fine tissue paper, fold two sheets together as one. This provides more resistance to the dye.

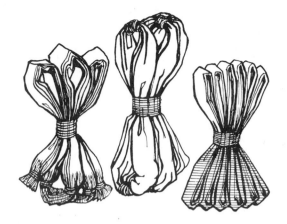

Two fine sheets of tissue paper dyed together

To make an interesting pattern with only one tie-up, fold the sample lengthways into four, six or eight or more thicknesses. Make into loops and tie in the centre. Dye each side a different colour. Then brush other colours on different areas. The samples must be bone dry before you undo them.

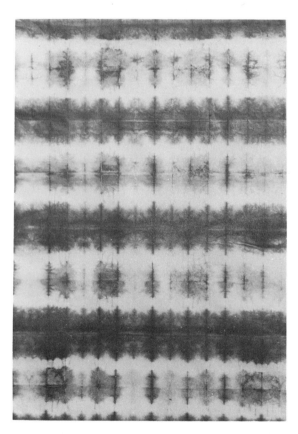

Tissue paper accordion pleated, made into loops, bound and dyed two colours

Information about dyeing, ironing, and sticking tissue paper will be found on pages 88, 97 and 100.

CRÊPE PAPER

Crêpe paper is soft and absorbent. Handle it carefully to retain the attractive crinkly appearance. When tie-dyed, its main uses will be for Christmas and party decorations, paper flowers, fancy dresses and hats (see cover and plates 27, 29 and 38).

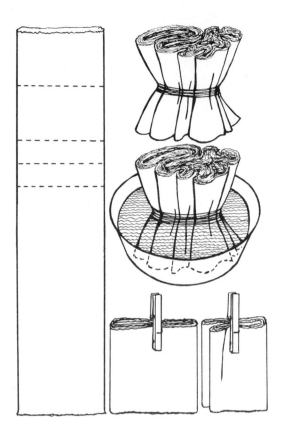

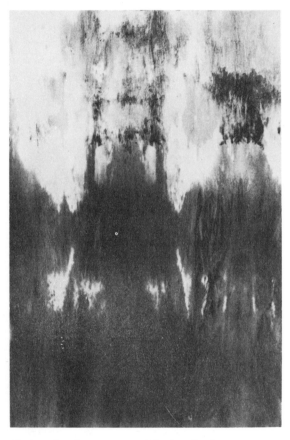

Strip of crêpe paper with dyed edges

For most purposes it is convenient to cut the roll of paper into horizontal strips or slices, and dye them in simple bands of different colours. Complicated bunching and folding methods are not successful with this stretchy paper.

Put a binding around the middle of the cut slice to form a bundle. Stand one side of the bundle, cut edges down, in shallow dye so

that the dye seeps upwards towards the central binding. Check to see that the dye has penetrated evenly on the inside folds of the bundle. Lift the bundle and drain or squeeze the excess dye at the side of the bowl (see page 96). Place it on newspaper to drain. Dye the opposite side of the sample a different colour. Pegs and clips can be put on the bundle instead of binding, and used to hold the sample while it is dip-dyed.

A wider slice of crêpe paper can have two bindings, dividing it into three sections (see binding over polythene, page 38). Dye each section separately in different colours.

The slices can be unrolled and made into loose loops. If the ends have been dipped in different dyes there will be alternating bands of colour along and across the strip of paper.

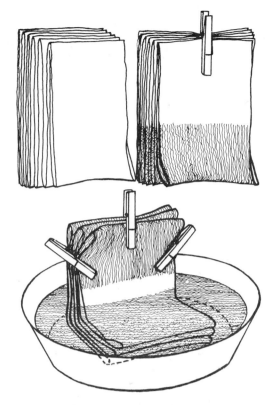

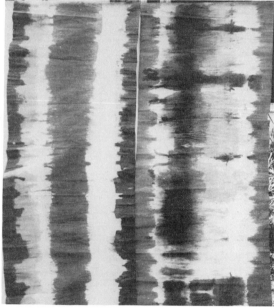

Stripes dyed across strips of crêpe paper

Whole rolls of crêpe paper dyed for making fancy dresses. These are very fragile when wet; do not bind or squeeze them. Make into a loose roll and dip in sections until a pleasing blend of colours is obtained.

An area in the middle of the crêpe paper can be left undyed or the colours may be allowed to intermingle. The latter gives an attractive effect worth aiming for. A shorter piece of crêpe paper can be made into accordion pleats (see page 65). Hold it with a peg while it is dipped in several colours.

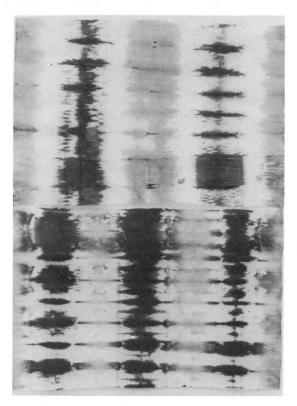

Small pieces of crêpe paper accordion pleated. Small pieces are easier to dye and there is less risk of tears.

After dyeing, drain and dry the samples in gradual heat. If dried too quickly, say, by a hot fire, the edges stick together, the paper tends to become brittle and there is even the possibility of scorching. Never try to undo the bundles until they are absolutely dry.

To straighten out the sample after drying, remove the pegs or cut off the bindings. Gently pat and spread out the drawn-in 'waist' areas made by the bindings. Press the bundle on both sides with a warm iron. Then unfold or unroll it and, using the iron sideways on, press the single paper very lightly in the direction of the crinkled texture. For a wide slice, place the paper, with the crinkly texture running horizontally, across a table or ironing board. Hold the top of the paper firmly on the table and slide the iron, held sideways on, from side to side. Work on a small section at a time until the bottom edge is reached. *Never* push the point of the iron forward into the paper.

If an iron is not available, quite large pieces of the dyed paper can be straightened out by gentle stretching. Find a piece of wood or hardboard a little longer than the width of the paper roll. Two people are needed; the first holds the paper firmly in both hands while the second slowly pulls the other end as he rolls it around the wood. This stretches the paper taut. Repeat the stretching in the opposite direction.

Smaller pieces of paper can be stretched by one person. Unroll the sample and place one end against the edge of a rectangular table. Press your body against the table to keep the paper taut while gently stretching and wrapping it round a piece of wood. Then unroll it and repeat the stretching in the opposite direction.

When the whole sample is rolled on the wood, put it on the table, flatten it with your hands and press it under a heavy book, or smooth the roll back and forth in the palms of the hands. Bad creases can be smoothed out by rubbing them with the index finger along the crinkled texture.

When the paper is not required immediately, wrap it in a tight roll and cover it with newspaper to protect the ends.

The edges of crêpe paper can be cut into fringes, scallops or points, or stretched or crimped. Practise with small pieces before tackling such articles as fancy dresses and hats.

GREASEPROOF PAPER

Greaseproof paper is inexpensive and tough. It is attractive when dyed in only one colour if the pattern is evenly distributed. It is strong enough to take a second or third dyeing. Its luminosity is an added bonus. When the light shines through the paper, the colours take on the brilliance of stained glass. This makes it ideal for mobiles.

Most tie-dye methods can be carried out in greaseproof paper. It can be marbled, folded, twisted, pleated and rolled.

Three panels of greaseproof paper, each folded in half across, then (top) pleated diagonally, (centre) folded into a triangle from centre and pleated, and (bottom) folded into a triangle to the centre and pleated

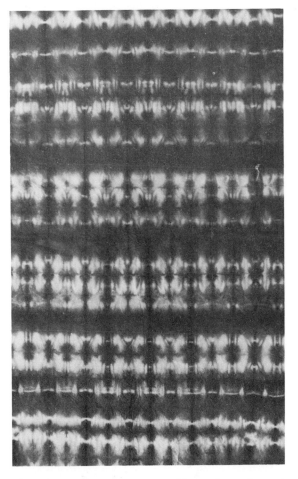

Greaseproof paper accordion pleated and bound at intervals

It is quite safe to undo greaseproof paper samples before they are dry. You may find little rivulets of dye have collected in the valley folds of the paper. If so, drain them away, dab them with soft tissues, place the sample between two sheets of newspaper and pat dry, or allow them to dry on the flattened surface of the paper.

When dyeing a second or third colour, rearrange, retie and put the sample in the next colour while the paper is still damp. In this way, a good strong colour can be obtained in 15–30 minutes.

To dye greaseproof (a non-absorbent paper) a deep, rich colour normally takes 2–4 hours or sometimes overnight. To reduce the length of dyeing time prepare

23

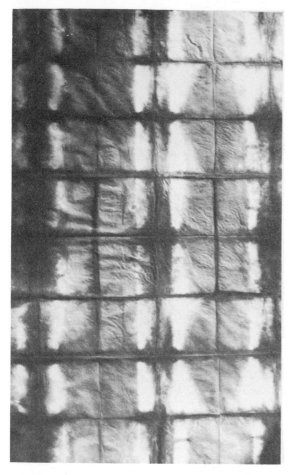

Greaseproof paper folded lengthways and across, soaked before dyeing and second colour dyed while still damp

the tied-up sample, but do not apply pegs, clips or binding. Soak the loose bundle in cold water for 30 minutes or, better still, pour boiling water over it and allow it to soak for 30 minutes. Squeeze or pat between newspapers, then apply the pegs, clips or binding, and dye immediately for 30 minutes or until a good strong colour is obtained.

CARTRIDGE PAPER

Avoid the thick 'woolly' types of cartridge paper. The finer varieties give more scope, as they are stronger and easier to manipu-

late. Spread out the folding lengthways on a large sample to keep the bundle as slim as possible. Smaller samples produce more interesting patterns.

Cartridge paper will fall apart at the folds if you try to retie and redye it several times. Therefore, the design must be achieved, where possible, with one main tying-up. Dip some areas of colour on the paper beforehand to give interest and variation (see page 88). Dry the paper before making the main tying-up. Do not leave corners or pieces of single paper projecting. Fold them inside or they might break away from the

Cartridge paper folded across and made into a bundle

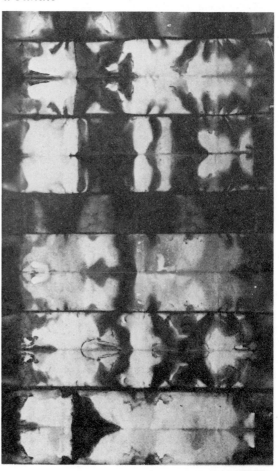

bundle when it is moved about in the dye (see page 62).

Folding is the most successful method to use with cartridge paper. When preparing the sample, do not crease the folds too severely. When the sample is soaked in the dye, any knife-edged creases tend to become weak spots and may split if treated

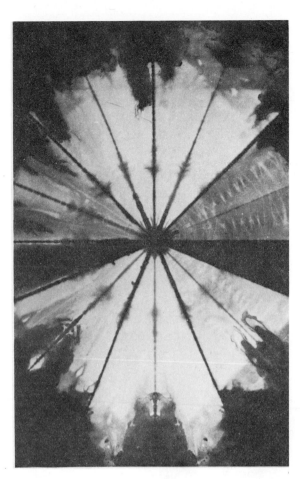

Cartridge paper folded into a dart shape and bound

Cartridge paper folded into quarters as D13 (page 59), then diagonally; pegs added

roughly. Crumpling, marbling and twisting should only be done loosely, if at all, and the binding put on sparsely. To get a good strong colour, dye the samples for 30 minutes–1 hour.

WALLPAPER

Quite often the cheaper wallpapers dye better than the more expensive ones. Usually the back of a patterned paper is the more suitable for dyeing, thus becoming the front of the tie-dyed sample. The cheap, plain paper used for lining walls and ceilings is very good, especially as backgrounds for collages and murals, or for making large articles.

This paper crumples quite well for the marbling and twisting methods, which are quick ways to pattern large samples. Small

Cartridge and wallpaper samples

quality, smoother paper, such as typing paper, is better than the cheaper, more spongy varieties, such as duplicating paper. It is strong enough to take a second tying-up and dyeing. Excellent designs are produced by folding the samples into fine accordion pleats, which can be parallel to each other or radiating from a point in a corner or on one side of the sheet of paper (see pages 65–68).

pieces of paper can be folded to give intricate and more precise designs, and if this kind of effect is required, it is advisable to tie-dye just the amount of paper needed for your particular project.

The stronger papers can be undone, retied and redyed a second colour. Try a preliminary colouring of the background as described on page 91. Dye for 30 minutes–1 hour.

TYPING, WRITING AND NOTE PAPERS

These papers offer a tremendous challenge to the skilful, accurate craftsman. Their size, texture and absorbency seem to be just right for creating the most striking designs in tie-dye. For precise work, the superior

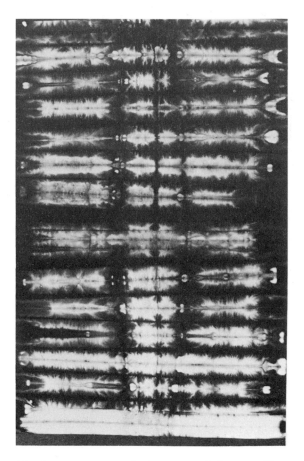

Typing paper made into parallel accordion pleats

Pegs, clips and rubber bands can be used. Finer threads and cottons are best for the bindings. String is too coarse for these exact, rather special samples.

Typing paper folded in half across, then pleated diagonally; rearranged for second colour. Rubber bands used as binding

Marbling and twisting methods can be used and are attractive, but *do* concentrate on the fine pleating techniques; you will be amply rewarded. Also try a series of very tiny squares or rectangles, 6–10cm (2½–4″) in size, folded in minute pleats. Dyed in brilliant colours, they give a jewel-like quality.

The length of dyeing time will vary from 30 minutes–4 hours, according to the bulk of the sample, the absorbency of the particular paper and the depth of colour required.

Try soaking some samples, or certain parts of them, in cold water for 5 minutes before dyeing. This produces a softer effect. The tie-dyed papers are greatly improved by hot ironing, first on the back and then on the front.

ENVELOPES

Envelopes of all types and colours dye exceptionally well, and provide an extremely cheap source of raw material. Those that arrive with the top flap just tucked in are a boon to tie-dyers. The tie-dyed, flattened-out shape of an entire envelope is rather attractive in its own right and is useful for many projects.

A collection of whole and parts of envelopes

Fold and dye used envelopes right side out, complete with stamp and address, or open them out and use the inside as the right side of the sample.

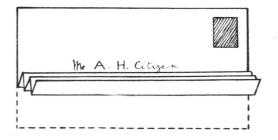

The envelope can be treated as a flat sheet of paper, or pleated as a folded-in envelope, whether or not it is turned inside out.

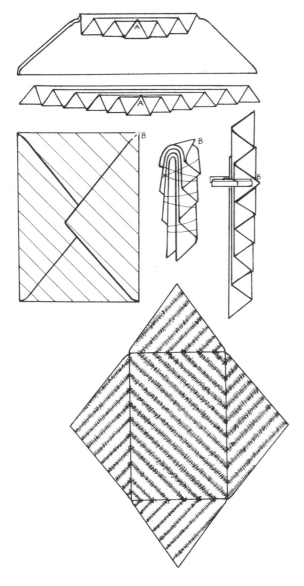

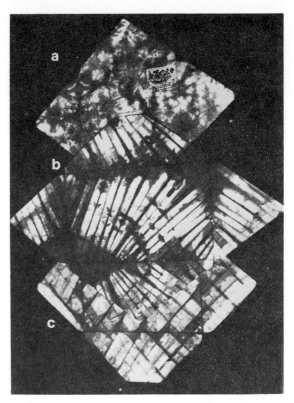

Three opened out tie-dyed envelopes: (a) marked with stamp and address, (b) pleated diagonally and dyed with flaps tucked in, then opened out, (c) plaid effect

The marbling method is very successful for all kinds of envelopes, although the folding and pleating techniques produce more attractive results. Spread the binding loosely along the whole length of the folded sample. Pegs, clips, rubber bands or pipe cleaners can be used. Open out, concertina-wise, any area of folding that lies between the pegs to allow the dye easy access to the inner folds (see page 67). Dye for 30 minutes–1 hour.

HAND-MADE AND SPECIAL PAPERS

When certain hand-made papers are tie-dyed, the results are extremely gratifying. Choose the fine to average weight, medium absorbent, pliable varieties. The very thick,

Make the pleats lengthways, across or diagonally. When the envelope is folded diagonally with the flaps tucked in, an unusual design is produced with stripes running in divergent directions. In every case after dyeing make sure that all flaps are freed while the sample is still damp.

spongy, brittle or harsh ones are not so successful.

The extra fine papers should be bound very tightly to preserve a definite resist area. Fine line bindings made with thread are particularly effective.

The following have been tested and are recommended, but there are many others that may give equally good results.

IMITATION JAPANESE PAPERS

All papers are approximately 50 × 75cm (20″ × 30″). This range, reasonably priced, is ideal for tie-dyeing.

No. 1   Semi-transparent, like fine tissue paper

No. 3   Like No. 1, but more substantial. Nos. 1 and 3 are very strong.

No. 6   Like fine cartridge paper; rough and strong

Nos. 4 and 8 Smooth and strong, the thickness of notepaper

Imitation Japanese paper no. 3 folded as D28 (page 61) and corners bound

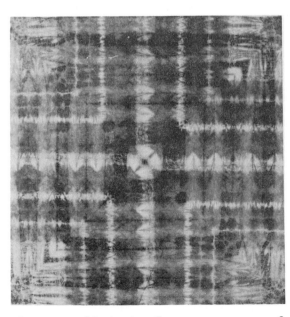

A square of imitation Japanese paper no. 3 folded as D20, then as D19 (page 60) and tightly bound

Imitation Japanese paper no. 3 folded into eight lengthways, the folds formed into small bunches at intervals and bound tightly

29

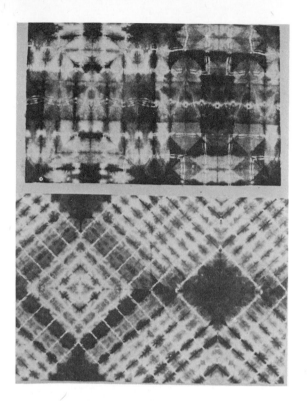

Imitation Japanese paper no. 3: (top) folded as D7, then the corners turned down and the whole accordion pleated and bound: (bottom) folded as D3 (page 58), then in half, accordion pleated diagonally and bound

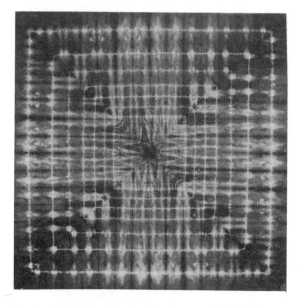

Imitation Japanese paper no. 3 folded as D22 and bound at intervals

REAL JAPANESE PAPERS

These are the cheaper and medium-priced papers from the range.

White Jap Tissue, semi-transparent, like ordinary tissue paper, but very much stronger

No. 2 More substantial than the tissue
No. 12 Opaque, medium thick
No. 15 Finer than No. 12, less opaque
No. 22 Thick and opaque, similar to fine cartridge paper

ENGLISH HAND-MADE

Hodgkinsons Medium White Wove 18lb HP (Hot Pressed)
Bodleian Repairing 22lb HP
Lens Tissue and also some printing papers

INDIA PAPER (English-made)

Thin, opaque and satin-like, 100×75cm ($40'' \times 30''$)

Schools and colleges should be able to arrange for their central supplies department to stock certain suitable types of hand-made paper for tie-dyeing. They can obtain supplies from manufacturers or wholesalers, who will usually sell in quantities of 500 sheets (one ream). Individuals requiring only small quantities of any one paper might persuade a local artists' materials or do-it-yourself shop to stock a selected range of hand-made or special papers for tie-dyeing.

English-made India paper folded lengthways. Points picked up at intervals along the fold and bound to give circular shape

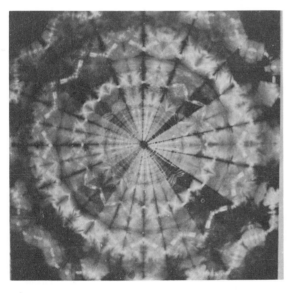

A square of Japanese paper made into a dart shape, folded diagonally at intervals with a binding made across each diagonal fold

PEGS AND CLIPS

Wooden and plastic spring pegs play an important role in tie-dyeing paper. They are an easy and effective means of keeping the sample in place. They are particularly useful in dip-dyeing because the peg can be held while the sample is dipped in the dye (see page 89). This makes them ideal for young children and beginners, while with skilful manipulation they produce some unique designs.

Paper kitchen towel folded into a dart shape; pegs added and dip-dyed

Paper napkin folded as D27, then as D20 (page 60); pegs added and dip-dyed

Paper kitchen towel folded lengthways and across; pegs added and dip-dyed

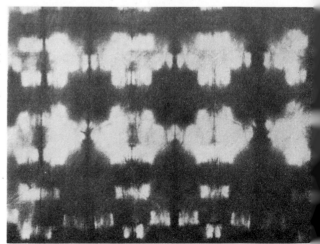

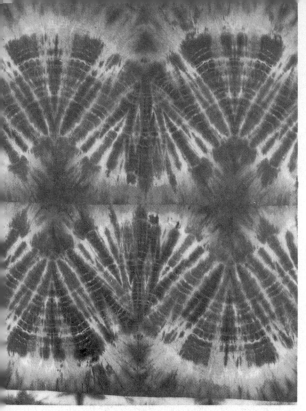

Double tissue paper folded in four across with irregular radiating pleats made diagonally

10 Single cartridge paper accordion pleated, the smaller with binding added, and the larger with pegs added

Japanese paper pleated lengthways and across and dyed twice to form a plaid pattern

12 Paper napkin dip-dyed in several colours

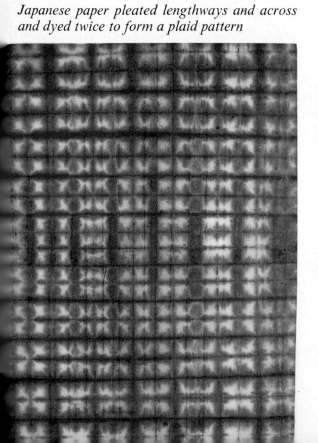

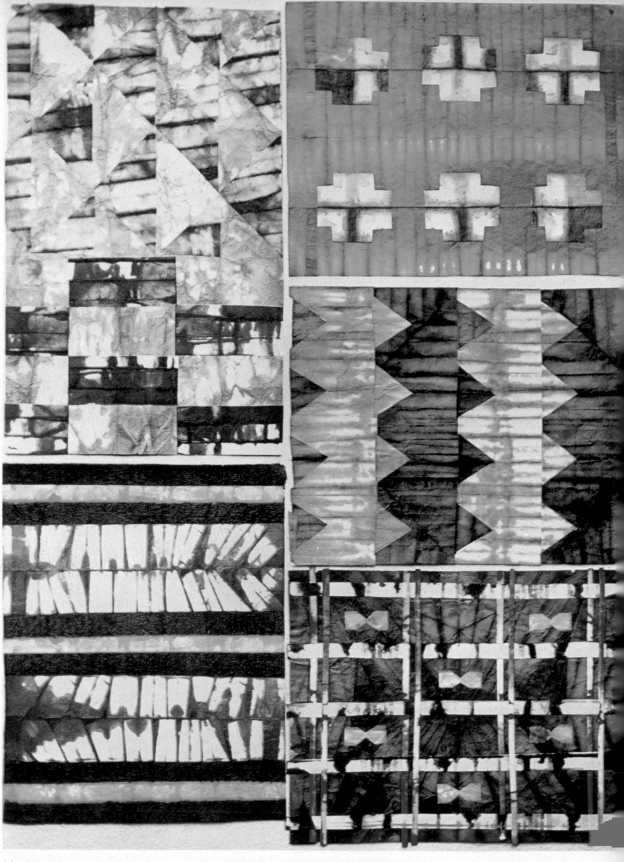

13　*Construction of patterns—stripes, plaid, spot, and counterchange*

Plastic pegs can be rinsed clean after being used. The wooden ones, even when washed, tend to retain some colour, which may be transferred to the next sample. This is not necessarily a disadvantage. When rinsing the pegs, open them so that the dye on the gripping surface is removed.

Whole sheet of tissue paper folded into four across, as D8 (page 59), then into a dart shape; pegs added on both sides

The slide-on type of peg can be used on medium absorbent papers, but on soft papers there is the risk of crushing and tearing the surface.

Many kinds of clips can be bought. Try out any that will grip the sample properly, whether they are wood, plastic or metal. Stainless steel letter clips are excellent.

When the paper is fragile, push the spring pegs and clips as far on the sample as they will go. This will stop them from sliding about or falling off when the bundle is in the dye. More important still, it will prevent any one peg or clip twisting over, taking with it a chunk of paper broken from the wet sample.

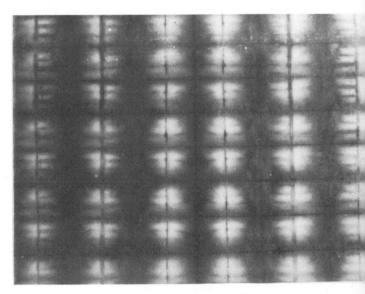

Tissue paper folded lengthways, made into a zig-zag bundle and pegs added

Do not use plastic pegs or clips in hot dye. This causes them to warp and lose their grip on the sample.

When pegs and clips are put on two or more sides of a sample, a flat, wide dye vessel is necessary. If the pegs and clips are all on the same side of a bundle, a narrower bowl with less dye is adequate because the paper can be immersed while the pegs project upwards above the dye. This applies particularly to long folded samples, which can be rolled into coils, or zig-zagged into a convenient-sized package to fit in the dye bowl. Secure the bundle with a little string.

33

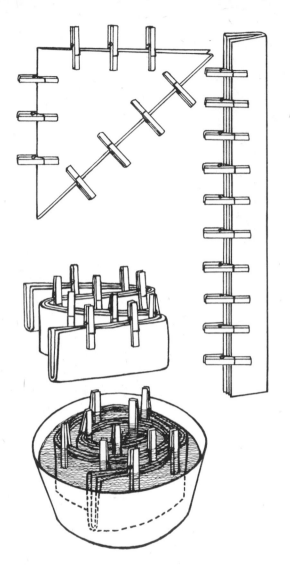

Tissue paper folded into four lengthways and four across, then folded over diagonally and pegs or clips added

Using the projecting pegs to lift the sample from the dye bowl makes it a much safer operation. There is no danger that the weight of the pegs will tear the fragile wet paper.

Slide-on paper clips can be tried on a very slim sample, but their use is very limited. They are troublesome to remove and may cause tears. Remove them when the sample is bone dry. Slide the lower edge of each clip sideways and up until it has moved through an arc of a quarter of a circle and the cut end is safely off the paper.

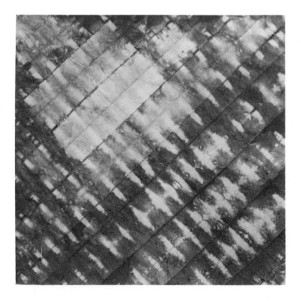

Shelf paper with background dyed, then folded into diagonal accordion pleats, zigzagged into a bundle and clips added

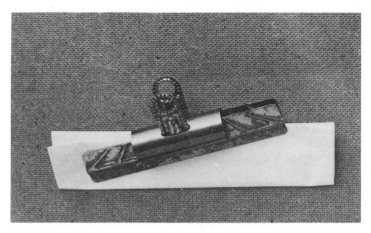

Whole sheet of tissue paper folded length-ways and across, with a very long bulldog clip added diagonally, and (below) the result

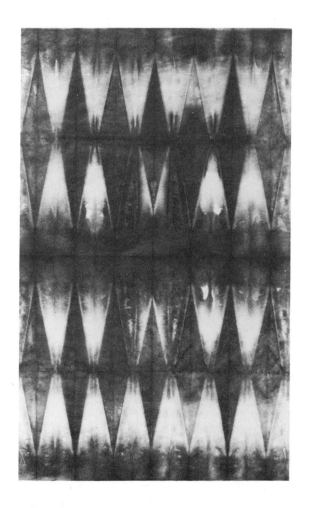

Whole sheet of tissue paper folded length-ways and across into a bundle, then folded over diagonally and three pegs added

BINDING

On the whole, binding does not play as important a role in creating a pattern in tie-dyeing paper as it does in tie-dyeing fabric. Its main function is to hold the bundle in place while it is being dyed. The ultimate design is decided by the size and absorbency of the paper, and the way the sample is folded or manipulated. This means that almost anything that is tied around a sample will serve the purpose, including all types of string, yarn, thread, raffia, etc. Split raffia into thin strands for small- to medium-sized samples, so that it does not cover too much of the outside area of the bundle, thus keeping out the dye.

Binding threads can be used over and over again. Rinse them before drying, then wrap them around a piece of cardboard.

Tear or cut old cloth into strips about 2cm ($\frac{3}{4}''$) wide, and roll or twist them for use on fairly large bundles. Cotton will tear into strips quite easily after an initial cut has been made on one edge. Cut old nylon stockings and tights into strips or, better still, cut them round in a continuous spiral about 2·5cm (1″) wide. When stretched, the strip will roll into a narrow tube that makes a cheap and good binding for large samples.

When the cloth and nylon strips are used by very young children, who find tying knots difficult, the two ends can be fastened off by twisting one round the other, making a half knot. This is sufficient to hold the binding while the sample is being dyed. In other cases tie the two ends together in a double knot.

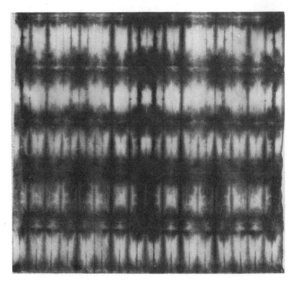

Tissue paper accordion pleated across and bound at intervals to give stripes

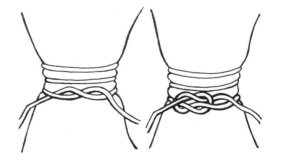

A BINDING WITHOUT TYING KNOTS

Place the thumb on the sample and put the thread or string under it, allowing 5–7cm

($2'' - 2\frac{3}{4}''$) of thread to hang loose. Wrap the working end of the binding thread round the sample several times, enclosing the loose end to keep it taut. Continue the binding as required. When finished, put a kirby grip over the cut end of the thread to hold it in place. In this way there is no need for a fastening-on or a fastening-off knot, making it much easier to undo the binding after dyeing.

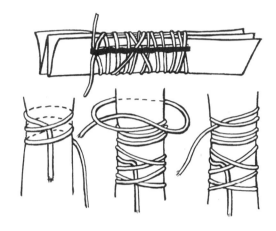

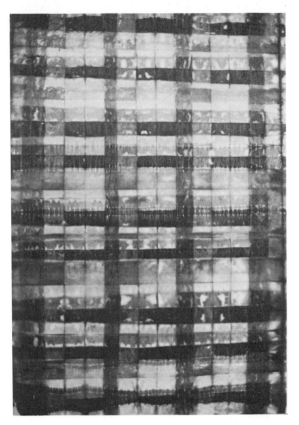

Florist's paper folded lengthways and across then wrapped round a thin piece of wood. Fine, close binding was added; dyed for 24 hours.

A SLIP KNOT

A slip knot made by tucking the loose end under the previous line of binding, as shown in the diagrams above, is another easy way to finish a binding.

A PRE-TIED SLIP KNOT NOOSE

When working with the handicapped and very young children who are unable to tie knots themselves, some pre-tied slip knots, prepared beforehand, are useful, especially when a small amount of binding is required.

Make a piece of string, approximately 30cm (12") long, into a loop or noose. Tie half a knot about 5cm (2") from one end and slip the other end through it. Tighten the knot so that the one end will slide backwards and forwards. Pull out a large loop in the centre. Wrap the loop around

the sample or a number of samples, then pull both ends away from each other. This tightens the noose and makes the binding firm. After the sample is dyed, the noose can be loosened, ready to use again, or cut.

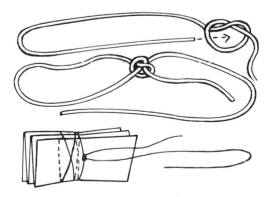

The tension of the binding should vary according to the type of sample and the design required. Leave the binding slack on medium to large, and thick, bulky samples, so that the dye can penetrate readily into the inner folds.

Make the binding tighter on small, thin bundles to retain some resist areas, on areas where the pleats are narrow or converge to a point, on samples where the paper is bound tightly round a base, and on long, thin samples where solid bands of thick binding are used to create a pattern of resist stripes (see page 67).

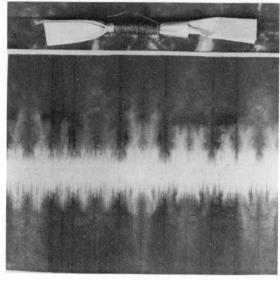

Pleated hand towel with polythene wrapped round centre and a solid tight binding added. This gives definite resist stripes on absorbent paper.

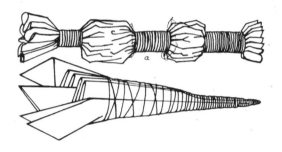

To assist in creating a wide resist band, wrap a strip of polythene round the sample several times and then apply a binding of string over it (see section *a* on the diagram above). This is particularly useful when dealing with soft, absorbent papers.

A definite 'binding texture' can be achieved on very small samples using firm paper, such as typing paper or bits from envelopes. Fold the sample into narrow pleats and bind fairly closely and tightly with thread along the length of the sample. Dye for 1 hour so that the dye can penetrate through the top layer of paper and dye a similar pattern on the layer underneath. This will not be as intense or definite as the top layer, but a paler, 'ghost' version of it. After drying and undoing, the best parts of the texture can be cut out from the rest of the sample and incorporated as special motifs and features in collages, etc.

MARBLING

This is a very easy technique, giving a varied, cloud-like or marbled texture that can be used for very many purposes. Practically every kind of paper, except the very brittle, will bunch up enough to produce some version of the method.

Marbling: (top) small sample, and (bottom) large sample

FOR SMALL PIECES AND SOFT PAPERS

Crumple and bunch up the paper into a ball in the palms of the hands, keeping the right side of the paper on the outside. Add binding, a string noose, rubber bands, pegs, clips, or pipe cleaners to hold the bundle together.

FOR LARGER OR HARDER PAPERS

Begin the crumpling from the corners, working in towards the centre gently and

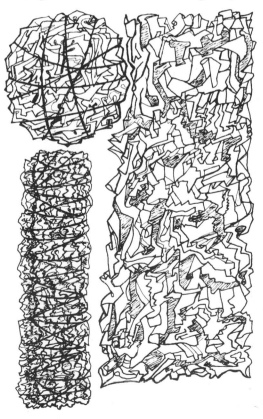

slowly. Then gradually squeeze in the sample to reduce the bulk. Fold in half lengthways. Bunch it into a sausage shape and bind.

The length of dyeing time will depend on the absorbency of the paper. A short dip is sufficient to colour a soft or small sample. Thirty minutes or more is needed for a larger or less absorbent sample. Drain, dry and undo.

If the paper is strong enough it can be tied up again, bringing the undyed areas to the outside of the bundle and tucking the well-dyed parts inside. Dye in a different colour.

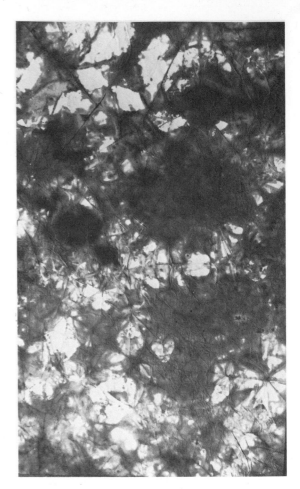

Marbling in two colours

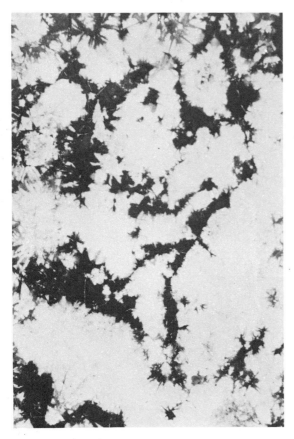

Marbling on florist's paper

Brittle papers are made more manageable and easier to crumple if first dampened by dabbing with a wet cloth.

Quite young children find marbling exciting and fun to do. If there is any difficulty in binding these samples, try pushing the crunched bundle of paper into the toe part of an old nylon stocking. Squeeze the stocking tightly over it and hold it in place with rubber bands or pegs, above and over the knob. Put more rubber bands on the paper knob itself if it is soft and absorbent, otherwise the dye will soak right through. If this should ever happen to a marbled sample, do not throw it away because the pattern is lost and there are no resist areas. Dry and undo the sample. Bunch it up again, putting on a much tighter and more compact binding than before to make the bundle firmer.

Then dip it for a few seconds in a darker dye or one of contrasting colour, or apply the dye to the outside surface with a brush.

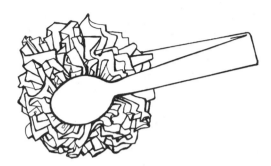

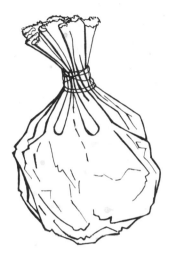

It is possible to hold a small crushed up bundle of paper in a pair of tongs (sugar tongs or those used by photographers), or squeezed between two small spoons, and to dip it in the dye for a short time without binding of any kind.

TWISTING

The twisting method is similar to marbling and is suitable for most types of paper.

Fold the sample lengthways or make it into a loose roll. Crush and squeeze it along the whole length to make it pliable. Hold an end of the crushed tube of paper in each hand and twist in opposite directions. Fold the twisted tube in half so that both ends are together. The rest of the sample will form into a coil. Secure the two ends with a peg, clip, rubber band or binding, and add more along the twisted coil.

A longer sample is best folded into several loops, each of which can be bound separately. The loops can be formed into a bundle with one binding around the middle. Each half can then be dyed a different colour.

Dip-dye or dye until a satisfactory effect is obtained. Drain, dry and undo. When the paper is strong enough, the sample can be retied and redyed, changing the position of the inner and outer areas to distribute the pattern to a wider area. After the first dyeing, the extreme ends can be dyed in a darker colour. Extra colour can be applied to the whole or parts of the sample with a brush. Where the dye has not soaked through too well, undo the binding or remove the pegs, then run a brush loaded with dye along the still crumpled sample.

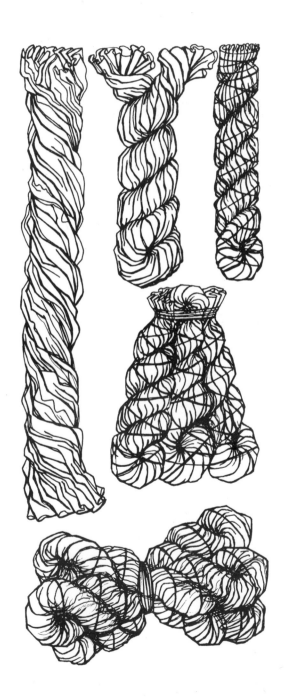

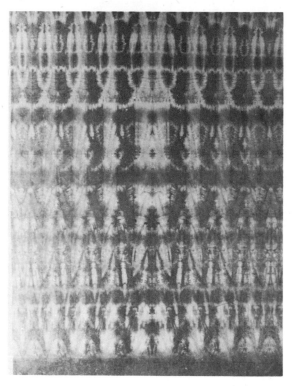

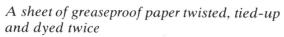

Twisting: sample made into loops

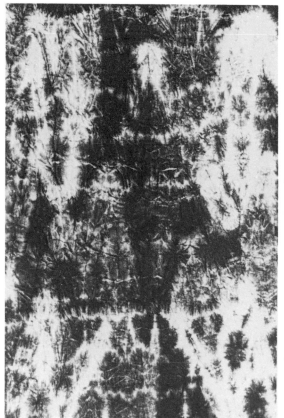

A sheet of greaseproof paper twisted, tied-up and dyed twice

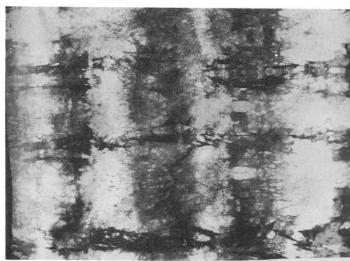

Paper towel twisted

ROLLING

Although it is easy enough to form most types of paper into rolls, this method has limitations. The reason for this is that, apart from the very absorbent papers, when a rolled-up sample is dyed, only the outer layers become coloured while the inner layers remain undyed.

To make the roll, place the single paper face downwards on the table. Roll the left side over to the right side. Add pegs, rubber bands or binding along the tube. Dye, dry and undo. For the second colour, roll the paper from right to left.

Roll absorbent papers closely and tightly so that the dye does not rush right through, and even fold the rolled tube in half or into four. The extreme edges of the sample, whether or not it is folded over, can be dipped in contrasting dye or have it applied with a brush. Dip-dye these samples for 5–20 seconds.

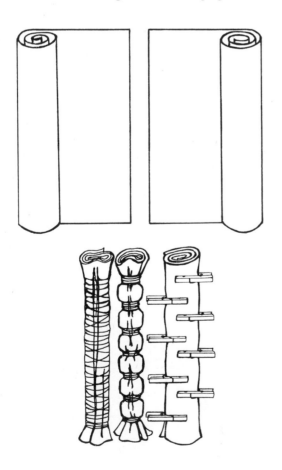

VARIATIONS FOR MEDIUM ABSORBENT PAPERS

Fold the paper in half. For the first colour, roll the cut ends towards the centre fold. For the second colour, roll the fold over to the cut edges.

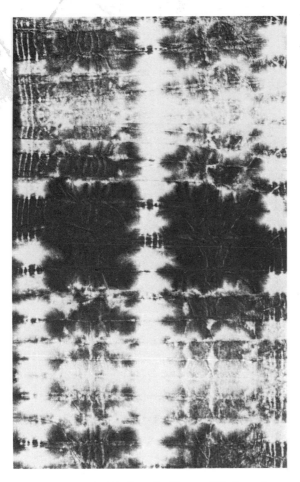

Section of shelf paper folded in half across, after the first dyeing. The fold was rolled over to the cut edges, then bound at intervals.

Paper towel folded in half across, the edges then rolled towards the fold; three areas of binding made

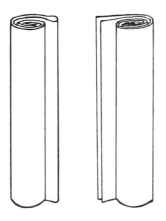

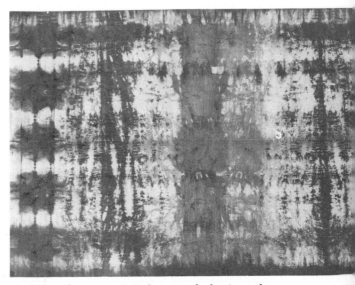

Result after rearranging and dyeing three times

Roll single paper in a diagonal direction, beginning at one of the corners, for the first colour. For the second, start the rolling from a corner that was on the outside of the tube. When the adjacent corner is used to begin the roll, the effect is different from that when the opposite corner is used. Roll double paper diagonally in the same way.

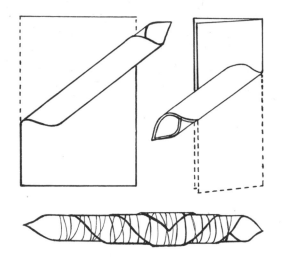

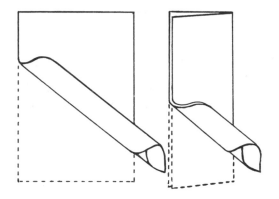

Paper towel rolled diagonally

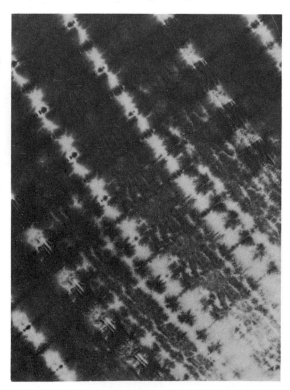

Roll both edges in towards the centre or fold the sides of the paper into the middle and roll the sample across or diagonally.

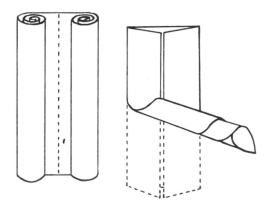

Roll single or double paper diagonally on a foundation of polythene. This is useful for paper that is not too strong. The polythene

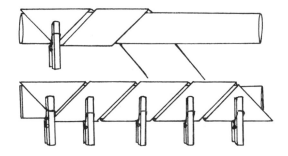

gives support to the rolled tube and is especially useful for tissue paper. If the tissue paper is folded into eight lengthways before rolling on the polythene and bound tightly at intervals, a zig-zag pattern is produced.

Form the sample into a cone by rolling it in a circular direction from a corner, or point along one side, or a fold made on the paper. Add binding, pegs or clips. The cone can be flattened and folded lengthways.

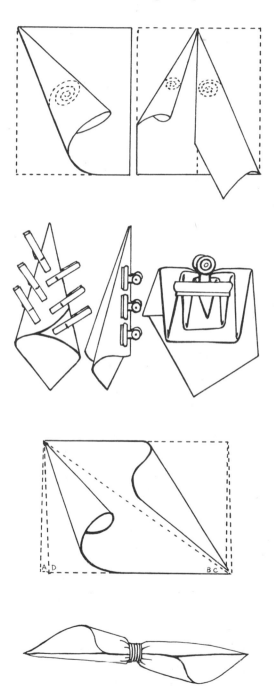

Tissue paper pleated into a tube and wrapped diagonally around polythene; bound to form zig-zags

Rolled on either side of a pivot point at the centre of the longer side

Florist's paper rolled into a double cone from diagonally opposite corners; bound at intervals

4 *Two counterchange designs using triangular shapes*

15 *Counterchange patterns*

6 *Cut outs: lace pattern and profile of a man*

17 *Collage*

18 *'Torrent', a collage*

WRAPPING PAPER ROUND BASES

The best bases to use for these methods are firm, rounded objects, such as tins, plastic containers, cotton reels, pieces of wooden dowel rods or wooden broom handles, even jam jars and bottles where the dyeing is done cold. The paper is wrapped round the base and bound very tightly to it so that the dye can penetrate only to certain areas, and this creates the pattern. Bases with flat areas of more than 4cm (1½″) allow the dye to seep under the binding into the paper, blotting out all resist areas. Pad these flat areas with wads of newspaper tied in place before applying the sample. The newspaper enables the string to get a tighter grip round the paper on the base, producing a more definite pattern. Do not leave in the dye too long.

Medium-size papers of medium absorbency give the best results, as the dye does not rush through too quickly. Soft absorbent papers are unsuitable. The exception to this is tissue paper. Fold into six or eight thicknesses before wrapping round the base, add extra binding and dye for 30 seconds.

Fold or roll the sample lengthways. Wrap it round the base:
(a) in layers, over and over itself;

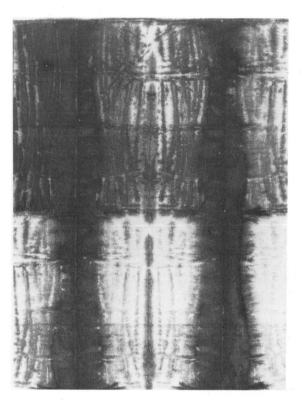

Tissue paper folded in half across and into four lengthways, then bound round a cylindrical case

(b) allowing a margin to extend beyond the base, projecting free of the binding;

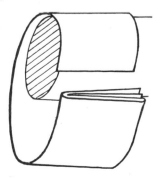

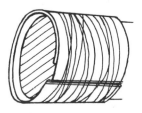

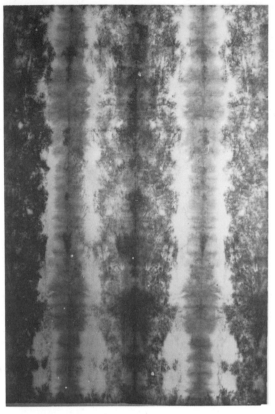

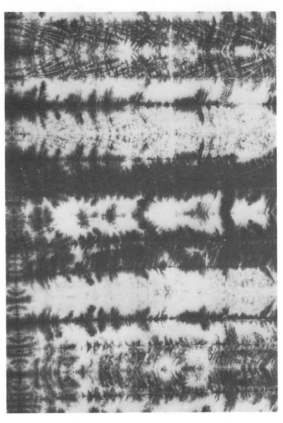

Sheet of tissue paper folded into four length-ways, and gathered round a broom handle, with some paper projecting. This was bunched up and bound.

Sheet of tissue paper folded in half across, then lengthways into a tube, wrapped loosely and diagonally round a base and bound

(*c*) in a diagonal direction so that one edge overlaps the other;

(*d*) into folds or gathers so that the tube of paper just fits round the base;

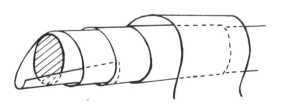

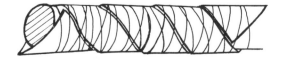

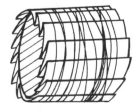

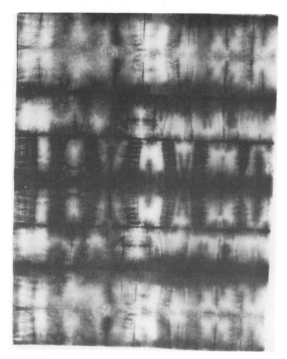

Sheet of tissue paper folded into eight, gathered loosely and bound round a piece of wood

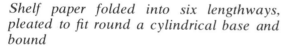

Shelf paper folded into six lengthways, pleated to fit round a cylindrical base and bound

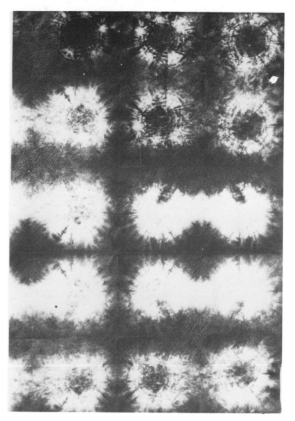

Tissue paper folded lengthways and across, then bound round the top of a bottle

(*e*) in a coil after making the tube into a twist.

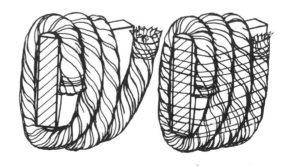

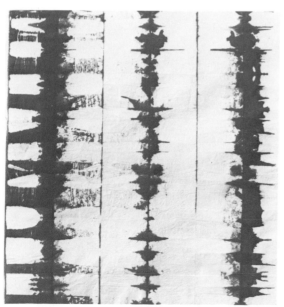

Slip on a rubber band to hold the sample in place. Then add a tight, compact binding of string. Remember it is this alone that must keep out the dye. If possible, concentrate the sample at one end of the base, as in diagram *b* on page 49. This means it can then be dyed in a smaller dye bowl. Have sufficient dye to cover the sample when the base is standing upright in the bowl. Leave it in the dye just long enough for the dye to penetrate to the inner layers of paper, without obliterating the pattern on the surface. Drain, dry and undo. If the sample needs a further dyeing, arrange the undyed parts on the outside, bind and dye in a different colour.

Lolly or ice cream sticks make good bases for very small pieces of paper (preferably not too absorbent). Fold the paper so that it is a little wider than the length of the stick. Roll the paper round the stick, and add binding, pegs or clips.

Crumple up a large sample as for marbling and place it over a base. The base can be an irregular shape, such as a chunk of cork or tree bark, a stone or a plastic article. Using string, raffia or cloth, bind the whole sample firmly and closely in all directions. Dye, drain and dry. Before undoing the bundle, try brushing a darker dye over the projecting sections in between the binding. Drain, dry and undo.

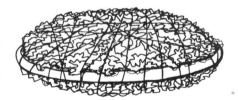

If a very large sample for a collage background is being patterned by this method and the bundle is too big to fit in your dye bowl, apply one or many colours with a brush over the whole surface. Make several applications of the dye to get an even penetration and a good strong colour.

A very long tube of twisted paper can be coiled or zig-zagged flat across one side of the base and bound very tightly. A second

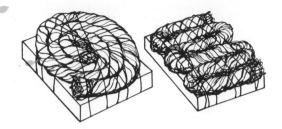

sample could be placed on the other side of a wide base so that with one binding the two samples would be tie-dyed at the same time.

Fold a small piece of paper like a closed umbrella in regular or irregular pleats, enclosing a lolly stick or pencil. Add pegs or close, tight binding over the whole or part of the sample. The folds of the paper can be twisted around in a downward direction before the sample is bound. To do this, place the centre of the paper over the top of the stick or pencil and hold the two together. Turn the stick over and over while

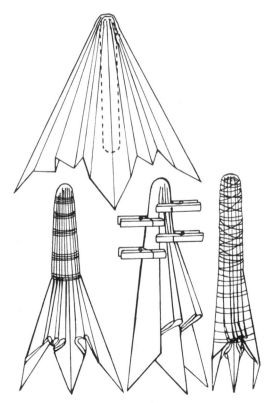

Paper towel pleated over a lollystick

the paper wraps around it. Dye the point at the top a different colour from the lower edges. This method produces an irregular circular design.

SANDWICHING PAPER BETWEEN WOOD

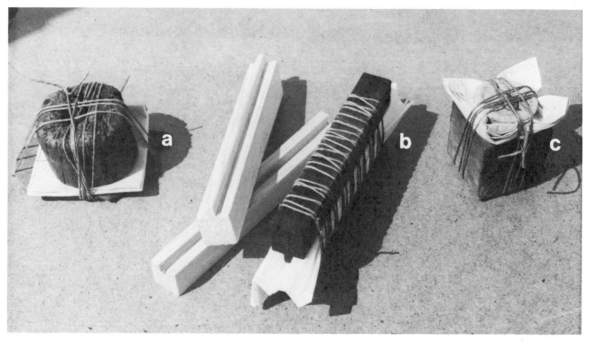

Ways of clamping a sample between two objects: (a) wood and cork with a hole, (b) two pieces of tongue and groove wood, (c) wood and a round rubber plug

Soft absorbent paper is not recommended for this method.

Find two thin pieces of wood, hardboard or plastic of similar size and shape. Lolly or ice cream sticks can be used for very small samples, and the wooden slats from date boxes are ideal for larger ones. Square or circular shapes, about 10cm (4″) across, produce different effects and should be tried.

Crumple, fold or roll the paper until it is slightly larger than the pieces of wood or plastic that will contain it. Place the pieces of wood on either side of the prepared

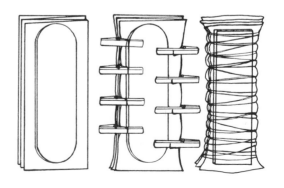

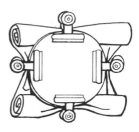

paper, in line with one another. Add binding or rubber bands along the whole length to clamp them firmly and tightly together. A thin bundle can be held together at intervals with pegs or clips.

Thicker hand-made paper folded lengthways and across, sandwiched and bound between two rectangular pieces of wood

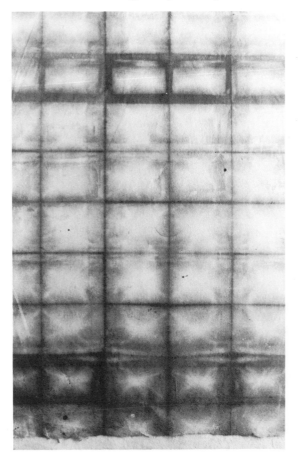

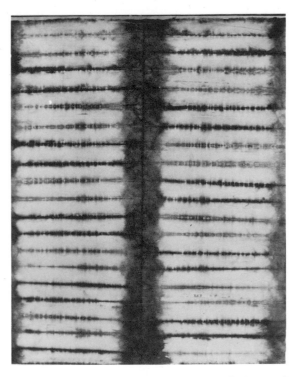

Thicker hand-made paper folded and sandwiched between two date slats, then bound

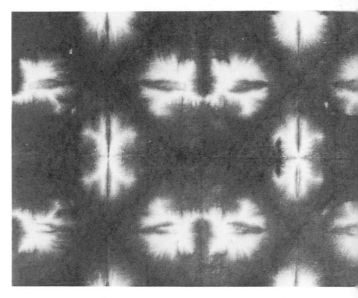

Hand towel folded into four lengthways and across, sandwiched and bound with the corners turned down

A flat, shallow dye vessel is required for these samples. Dye for 30 minutes–1 hour. Try brushing extra colour on the projecting parts. The sample can be refolded in a different way, sandwiched and bound, then dyed in a second colour.

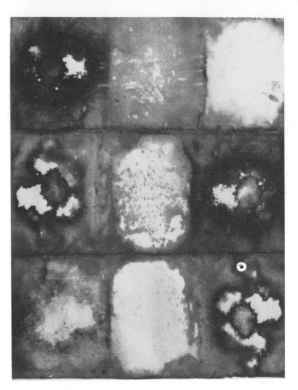

Cartridge paper folded and sandwiched between wood and a cork with a hole. A darker dye was added through the hole in the cork.

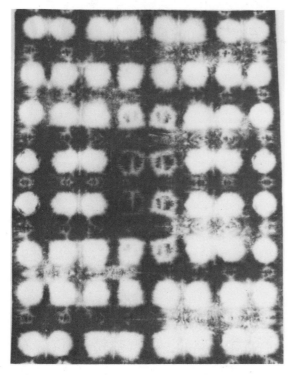

Sheet of tissue paper folded, then sandwiched and bound between wood and a circular plug, as in photo on page 54

Here are some variations on this method.

(*a*) Sandwich folded or pleated paper between two pieces of wood or plastic that are dissimilar or of irregular shape.

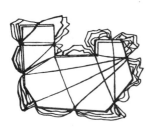

(*b*) One piece of wood can have a hole in it through which the dye has access to the sample, giving unusual patches of colour. A second colour can be infused through the hole or holes.

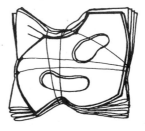

(*c*) Sandwich a compactly folded paper at one end of the pieces of wood, allowing it to jut out some distance. Leave the projecting area fairly loose, or arrange for the binding to bunch it up haphazardly, close to the sandwiching boards.

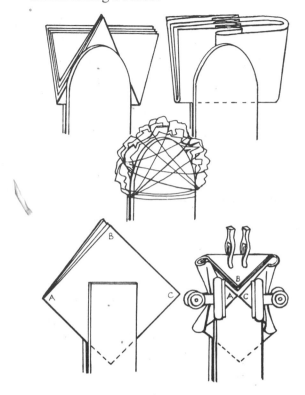

Sheet of tissue paper folded, clamped diagonally and bound between two pieces of tongue and groove wood

Sheet of tissue paper folded, clamped and bound between two pieces of tongue and groove wood

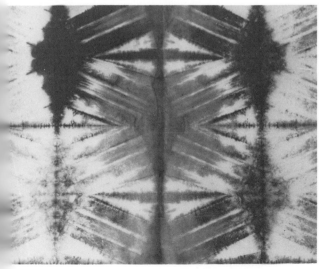

FOLDING AND PLEATING

Folding is the most important technique, producing varied and beautiful designs. It is suitable for all kinds of paper. Small, fine-textured papers can be folded precisely and accurately, whereas larger, coarser ones can be treated more casually and folded irregularly. Whether a sample of any kind or size is folded precisely or at random, it acquires a character of its own. This fact should encourage the beginner to try a few easy experiments. With skilled handling and careful workmanship, jewel-like specimens can be created, complete and satisfying in themselves.

When preparing your samples, avoid putting too much pressure on the turned-over edges of folds and pleats, unless the paper is very strong and resilient. Knife-edged creases tend to cause weak spots and even splits, particularly on spongy paper, after being immersed in dye for some time. To minimize this danger, handle the samples gently, do not pack them in the dye bowl too closely together and do not move them about once they are in the dye. Be sure they are bone dry before undoing them.

1   A rectangle ABCD, O the centre point

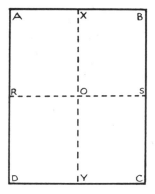

2   Folded in half across

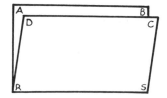

3   Folded in half across with sides to the middle

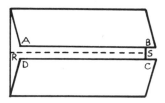

4   Folded in half lengthways

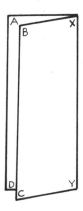

5 Folded in half lengthways with sides to the middle

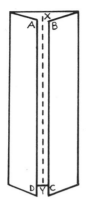

6 Folded in half, then into four

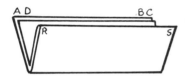

7 Folded into four with centre fold inside

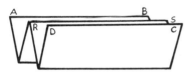

8 Folded into four with centre fold outside

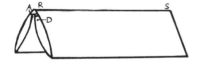

9 Folded in half, then into three, giving six thicknesses

10 Folded in half, then into four, giving eight thicknesses

11 Mountain (M) and valley (V) folds

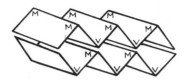

12 A square ABCD, with O the centre point, folded in half

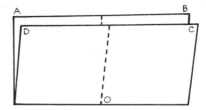

13 Square folded into quarters

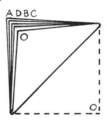

14 Square folded into quarters, then into a triangle, with the centre point O taken over diagonally to the outside corners

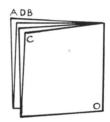

15 Square folded into quarters, then into a triangle by making a diagonal fold across from the centre point O

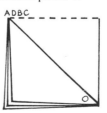

16   A square folded across both its diagonals and opened out

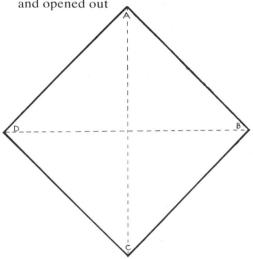

17   A square folded in half diagonally

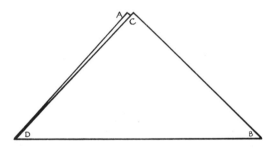

18   As 17, with the apex of the triangle taken over to the centre point on the diagonal fold (four thicknesses)

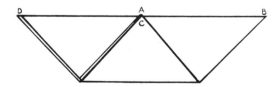

19   As 17, but folded over to give eight thicknesses

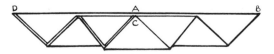

20   Square folded into quarters diagonally

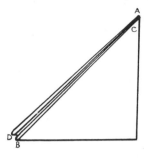

21   As 20, then folded over in half

22   As 20, then folded over into four

23   Square folded in half with outside corners turned down diagonally to meet in the centre

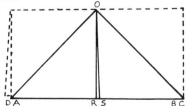

24 As 23, then the outside folds brought into the centre (to form a dart shape, fold back in half)

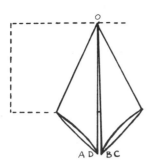

27 A square with the corners folded over diagonally so that they meet in the centre

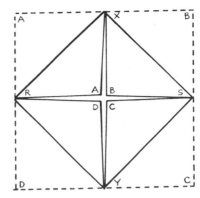

25 As 24, then folded back in half and the top layer opened out

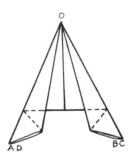

28 As 27, with the corners of the newly formed square folded over again diagonally to meet in the centre

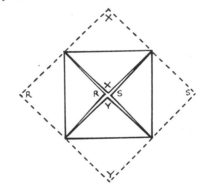

26 As 24, then the outside folds brought inwards to meet in the centre (fold back in half to make a narrow dart shape)

29 As 27, then folded back in half

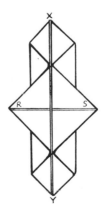

30 As 29, but folded back in half with corners meeting at the centre fold

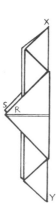

31 As 29, then folded back into four with the corners meeting at the centre fold

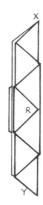

As a preliminary to all folding techniques, make it a standard practice to begin by folding the paper in half, right side out, lengthways, across, or diagonally (see pages 58–60). Then fold or pleat in the method chosen. This ensures that the right side of the paper always comes on the outside of the tied-up bundle. Sometimes the edges of the paper come on the outside of the bundle. Then the effect is rather wasted because the best part of the pattern is created on the outer edges of the sample.

To spread out the pattern when any cut edges come on the outside of the bundle,

turn them in once or twice as if making a hem. Sharp corners can be turned inwards in the same way.

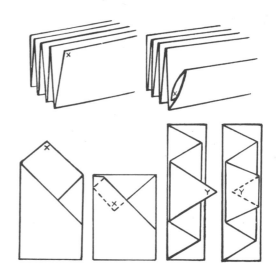

Shelf paper folded into four lengthways and across, then diagonally; dyed two colours

Greaseproof paper folded into a dart shape, bunched and bound tightly. M and V folds reversed for second colour

When you have completed the folding, hold the bundle in place with pegs, clips, rubber bands or binding, or a combination of these. Rubber bands are really only suitable for short bundles, as they can only be placed at either end. It is more difficult to stretch them along the middle of a longer sample. Bindings need not be pulled too tightly, except where a resist area is planned (see page 38).

Medium absorbent papers that are not too thick and have a firm, fine texture, such as typing paper, shelf paper, florist's paper, hand-made paper, etc., are ideal for these methods. Tissue and greaseproof papers also give very rewarding results.

Mountain and valley folds are referred to on the diagrams as **M** and **V**. Mountain folds are convex and point upwards; valley folds are the concave creases in between the mountain folds. After dyeing a folded sample, dry and undo it. Reverse the mountain and valley folds. Bind and dye a second colour. This distributes the pattern over a wider area.

Fold small and medium samples in any of the ways shown in the preliminary and basic folding methods (pages 58–62). Add pegs and clips before dip-dyeing or dyeing. If binding is used, make some extra pleats to reduce the sample into a narrower bundle.

SIMPLE STRIPES

Fold the sample lengthways in two or four. Pleat across to form a narrow bundle.

Japanese paper made into a rectangular bundle, folded over diagonally and a clip added

63

Put a binding round the middle, or hold with a peg, and dye each side a different colour. Dip the edges in an extra colour or apply it with a brush.

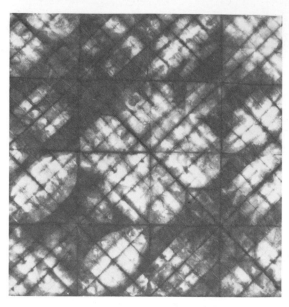

Shelf paper folded as D27–30 and pleated before being bound

Folded into six across, as D9, pleated into a bundle and bound

Shelf paper folded as D27 and pleated before being bound

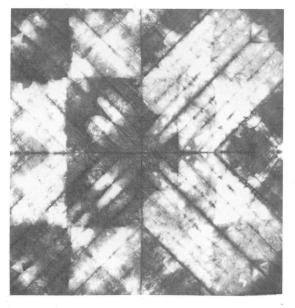

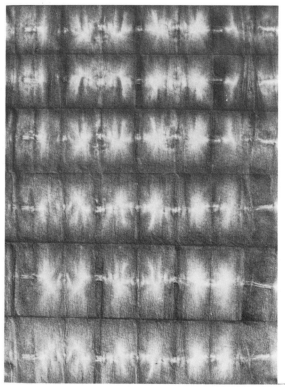

19 *'Fir trees and lake,' collage composed from triangles and rectangles only*

20 *'Footballers,' collage with figures cut from tie-dyed envelopes*

21　Dressed paper dolls

22　'Planet trekker,' model covered with oddments of tie-dyed paper

23　Cat and Owl hand puppets, Farmer's Wife string puppet, all made from tie-dyed paper bags

24　Mr Funny Face, hand puppet from tie-dy[e] paper bag

25   *Shepherdess hat*   26   *Picture hat, front view showing patchwork effect*

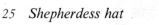

Picture hat, back view

28   *Floral crown*

29 *Flowers made from various tie-dyed papers*

30 *Foliage*

31 *Flowers made from tissues and paper napkins by children four and five years old*

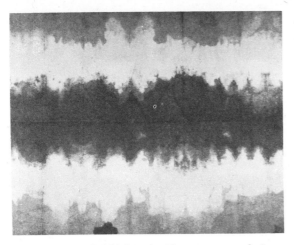

Paper towel folded in half across, made into a bundle, bound in the middle, and each side dyed different colours

Paper towel folded into four across, made into a bundle, bound in the middle, and each side dyed a different colour

MULTI-STRIPES: ACCORDION PLEATS

When the paper is made into a series of accordion pleats, the edge of each fold receives the dye and so becomes a stripe. There are two ways of making accordion pleats. In each case begin with the paper folded in half.

Forwards and backwards method Turn over the folded or cut edges for the first pleat. Crease lightly. Pick up the newly formed fold with both hands and flick the remainder of the sample forwards towards your body. Make a new crease to form a second pleat parallel with the first.

Pick up the double pleats and flick the rest of the sample backwards, away from the body. Lightly crease the new pleat. Continue in this way, making a fresh pleat with each flick of the paper forwards and backwards, until the whole is formed into a bundle of equal, parallel accordion pleats. Tuck the outside cut edges inside the adjacent pleat.

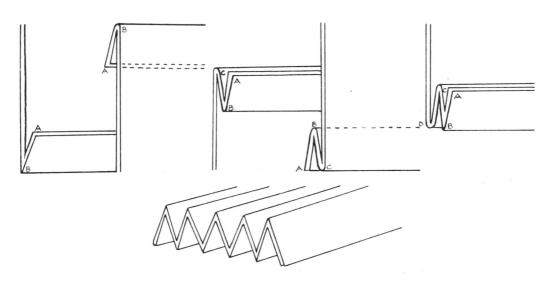

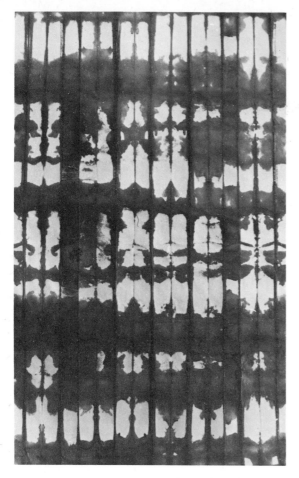

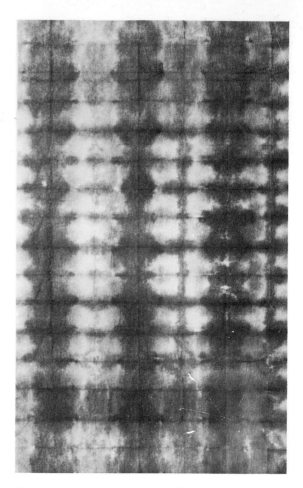

Typing paper accordion pleated and bound

Greaseproof paper accordion pleated and bound at intervals

Mountain fold method This makes slight guideline creases for the pleats. Fold the sample lightly into four, six, eight or more until the tube of paper is twice the width of the proposed accordion pleats.

Reverse all the valley folds, making them into mountain folds.

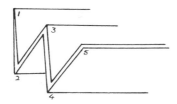

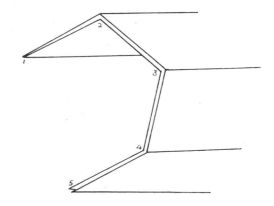

Unfold until the sample is folded in half. There are now mountain and valley folds.

Turn the folded edge over to the nearest mountain fold and crease lightly.

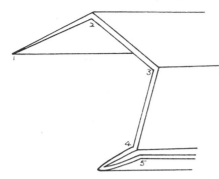

Pick up the folded edge and the nearest mountain fold together in both hands and take them over to the next mountain fold. Crease.

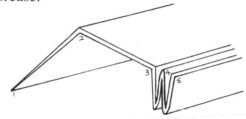

Shelf paper accordion pleated lengthways, folded across, and bound

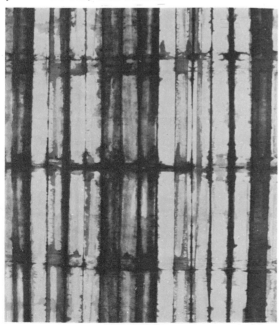

Continue in this way until all the mountain folds are collected together and the bundle of accordion pleats is complete. Tuck the outside cut edges inside the adjacent pleat (see page 62). Add pegs or loose binding.

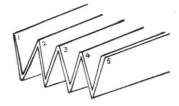

For stripes across the sample, make 'waists' and add solid taut bindings at intervals. Spread out the pleats concertina-wise in between the bindings.

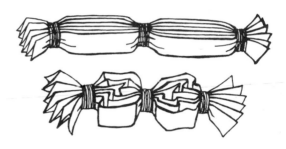

Japanese paper bound closely to give a stripe along the edge of each accordion pleat

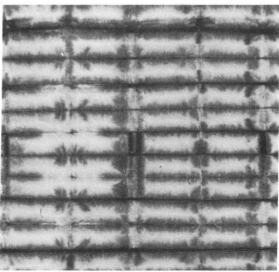

RADIATING AND IRREGULAR PLEATS

In this method most of the pleats vary in width. They are often wider at one end than the other and they are not made in parallel rows. Where several pleats are narrowed off at one point, the direction of the pattern changes, swinging round as in the segment of a circle. When two or more swings are made in opposite directions on one sample, an interesting S-shaped design is produced.

Begin the folding on any of the four sides of a sheet of paper that is doubled over, but not necessarily in half. Form the pleats by the forwards and backwards method (see page 65). Vary the shape and width of each pleat as the design requires. To change direction, gradually straighten the pleats so that they are the same width at both ends. Then begin the reverse swing by making the pleats narrow at the formerly wider end, and wider where they had previously been narrow.

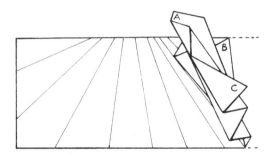

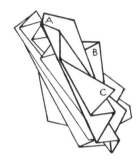

Thin, strong paper folded in half lengthways and made into irregular radiating pleats

Greaseproof paper accordion pleated diagonally

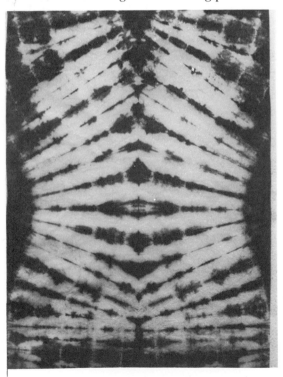

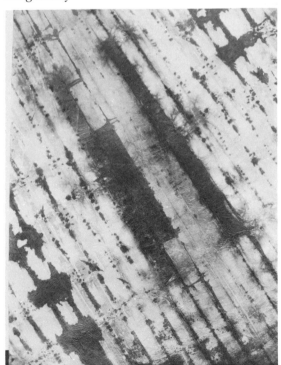

DIAGONAL AND CHEVRON ACCORDION PLEATED STRIPES

Fold a square or rectangle of paper in half diagonally. Form it into accordion pleats parallel with, or at right angles to, the halfway fold. This automatically produces pleats in a diagonal direction. If the pleats are at a slight angle to the halfway fold, some semblance of a chevron pattern will emerge.

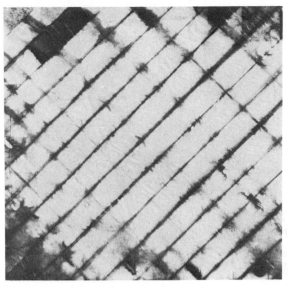

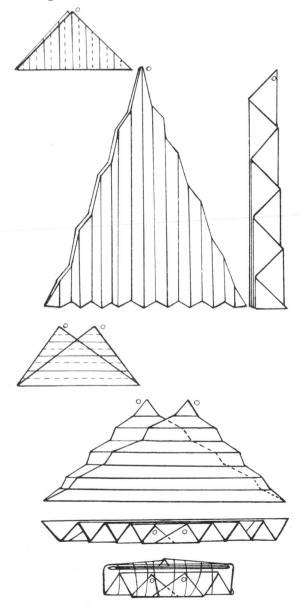

Greaseproof paper accordion pleated diagonally, closely bound to give dyed stripes only on the edges of the folds

To produce a regular chevron pattern, fold the paper in half lengthways or across. Beginning at one of the corners, make accordion pleats diagonally across the sample.

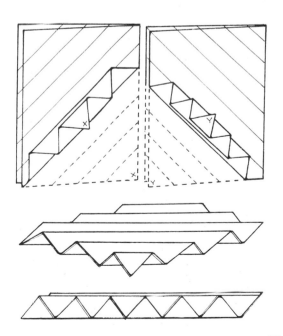

Japanese paper folded into four lengthways, then made into diagonal accordion pleats. Close binding added to give a skeletal effect

Greaseproof paper folded in half lengthways, then accordion pleated diagonally to give a chevron effect

Right: greaseproof paper folded in half across and pleated diagonally; dyed two colours

Typing paper folded in half lengthways and made into diagonal accordion pleats; dyed one colour

As previous photo, but M and V folds reversed before dyeing second colour

When using absorbent papers, fold the sample into four, six or eight thicknesses before making the diagonal accordion pleats.

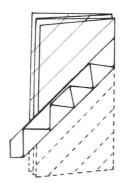

To produce a zig-zag design make taut narrow bindings at intervals along the bundle. For a second dyeing of the chevron

pattern, reverse the mountain and valley folds.

Most of these accordion pleated samples give very interesting effects if the initial folding in half is done with the sides turned in to the middle.

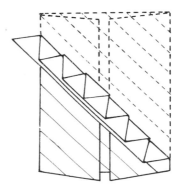

Imitation Japanese paper no. 3 folded into four across, and three lengthways, then the bundle accordion pleated and bound at intervals

Imitation Japanese paper no. 3 folded in half lengthways, and into six across, then made into diagonal accordion pleats and bound at intervals

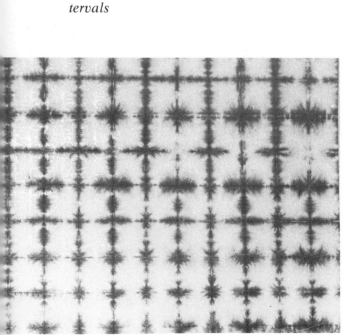

Left: tissue paper accordion pleated lengthways, then the tube zig-zagged across to form a square bundle and bound; one dyeing

PLAIDS

For a plaid design, make the preliminary fold in half across the sample and then form into parallel accordion pleats. Dye the first colour. Dry and undo. For the second colour, make the preliminary fold in half lengthways and make parallel accordion pleats.

For a diagonal plaid, work in the same way, making the preliminary halfway fold and pleats for the second colour at right angles to those for the first colour. This means that both the diagonals of the square or rectangle are used as preliminary halfway folds.

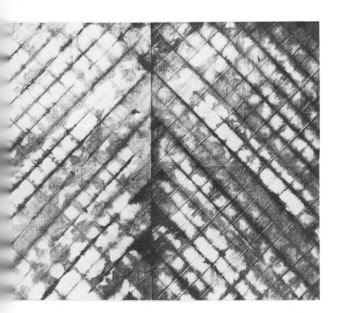

Florist's paper accordion pleated to form diagonal plaid

PIVOT PLEATING: SINGLE PAPER

In each case, after pleating add pegs, clips or sparse binding before dyeing.

On a single rectangular sheet of paper ABCD, fold the shorter side AB down towards the longer side AD in small radiat-

ing pleats, using corner A as the pivot point.

Pivot pleat the paper on either side of X, the centre point of the shorter side AB, until the two bunches of pleats meet in the centre. Turn them back to back.

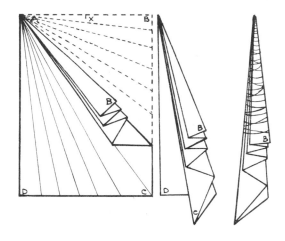

Single cartridge paper, shorter side pivot pleated down to longer side

Work in the same way using S, the centre point of the longer side BC, as the pivot point.

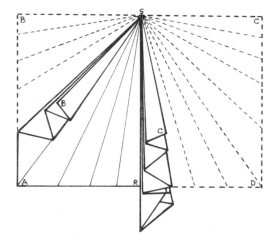

Typing paper pivot pleated down from both sides of the centre point along the shorter side

Fine cartridge paper pivot pleated down from both sides of the centre point along the longer side

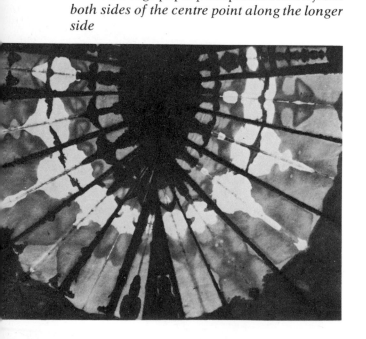

These two items could also be pivot pleated on double paper by folding in half beforehand.

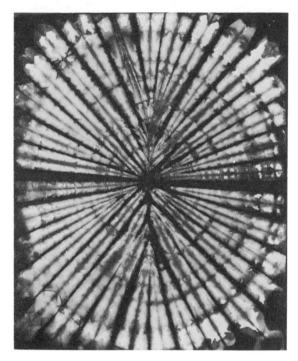

Typing paper folded in half across, then pivot pleated down on either side of the centre point on the fold

As previous photograph, but pivot pleating made from the centre point of the shorter cut edges

PIVOT PLEATING: DOUBLE PAPER

Fold a square or rectangle of paper ABDC into quarters to give the centre point O and centre line XOY. If guidelines for creases are needed, keep folding the paper in halves until an arrow shape is formed.

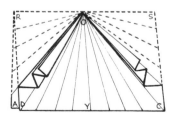

Open up the sample to the halfway fold. Make into all mountain folds. Beginning at the centre of the fold and using O as the pivot point, form the right-hand side of the sample into small radiating pleats, finishing at the centre line OY. Hold in place with a peg. Pleat the left-hand side down in the

same manner. Turn the two pleated halves back to back, making a narrow, pointed bundle. Add pegs, clips, rubber bands or binding.

VARIATIONS ON PIVOT PLEATING

Turn the sample round so that the cut edges are at the top. Then use X as the pivoting point instead of O, folding the cut edges down towards the fold.

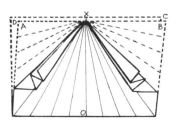

Use a pivot point that is off centre along the centre fold or on the cut edges.

On a sample that is more than twice as long as it is wide when folded in half, fold the two top corners over to the lower edge RS and crease. Use the two points P and Q, where the creases cross the top edge, as pivot points. Make small pleats radiating from the two pivot points P and Q until they are vertical at R and S. Pleat the gap in between the two groups of pleats so that the sample forms a bundle with all the pleats meeting in the middle. R and S can also be used as pivot points.

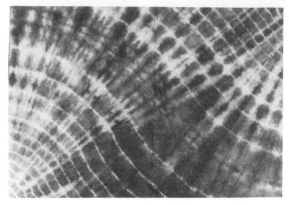

Imitation Japanese paper no. 3, the two shorter sides pivot pleated from opposite corners in towards the central diagonal line

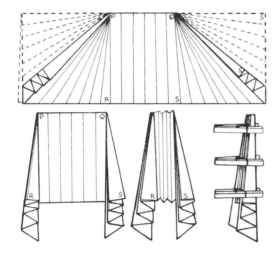

Folded in half across, then as previous photograph. This produces a positive and reverse effect of the pattern.

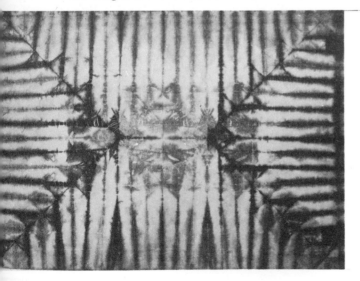

Tray cloth of Japanese paper folded so that the length is more than twice the width

On single or double paper pleat both short sides towards the centre line OX.

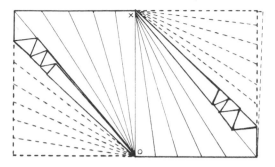

Make pivot pleats from diagonally opposite corners X and Y until they meet along the imaginary diagonal between the two corners.

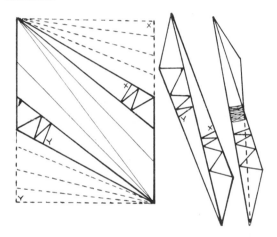

Fold corners B and D in towards the diagonal AC. Use A and C as pivot points from which to pleat the sample lengthways or across.

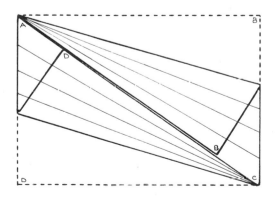

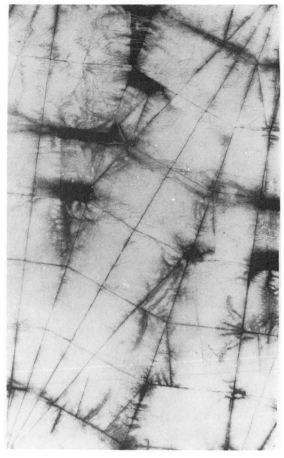

Greaseproof paper folded from diagonally opposite corners, and then across

Typing paper folded diagonally and pivot pleated

All the methods mentioned above can also be carried out if the preliminary folding in half of the paper is done by bringing the sides to the middle. This produces changes in the usual direction of the pleats and, thus, in the final design.

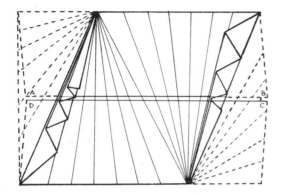

Thin, strong paper folded in half diagonally; the two sides then pivot pleated from the top corners down towards the centre of the fold

Pivot pleat from the centre of a diagonal fold.

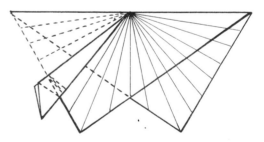

Fine resilient paper folded into three length ways and six across, then pivot pleated from opposite corners in towards the imaginary diagonal

Small to medium samples are best bound with thread or cotton, larger ones with fine string. Make the binding firmer and closer where the pleats are narrow, and looser on the wider parts. For a second dyeing, reverse the valley and mountain folds. Bind and dye. Adjust the dyeing time according to the bulk of the sample and the absorbency of the paper.

DENTING IN THE CORNERS OF FOLDS

This little trick helps to extend the dyed part of a fold and at the same time gives a bonus in the form of a diamond- or star-shaped design. The fold should be more than 2·5cm (1″) wide to give enough room for the denting to be done properly. Make a diagonal crease across one corner of a not too bulky fold. Straighten it out. Push the corner inside the fold along the diagonal creases. Press. This will now stay in place without adding pegs or binding.

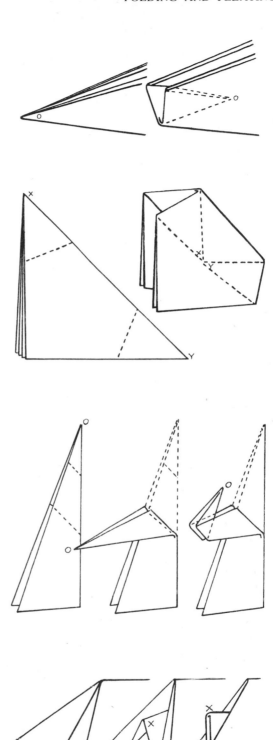

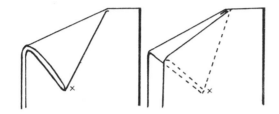

Where there are several such folds together, treat all the corners in a similar manner. Do not try to force in the corners where folds are too narrow or bulky.

Make a series of wide folds. Bind them in the middle or add pegs. Dent each of the folds on both sides, or on all four corners. Folds that come to a point will also dent inwards.

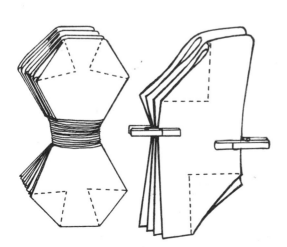

Thin strong paper folded into a square bundle, the sides dented in and a peg added

Folded into four, then into a bundle and corners dented in

Fold the sample lengthways, then across into a square bundle ABCD. Fold the A corners down diagonally to the corner folds at C to form a set of right-angled triangles. Add a clip or binding.

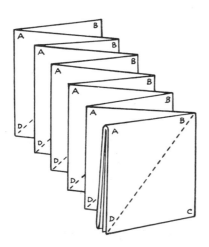

'*Magic garden*' collage by children 6 to 8 years old

Another part of the 'Magic garden'

35 'Dogs'

34 'Cats,' cardboard models covered with tie-dyed paper

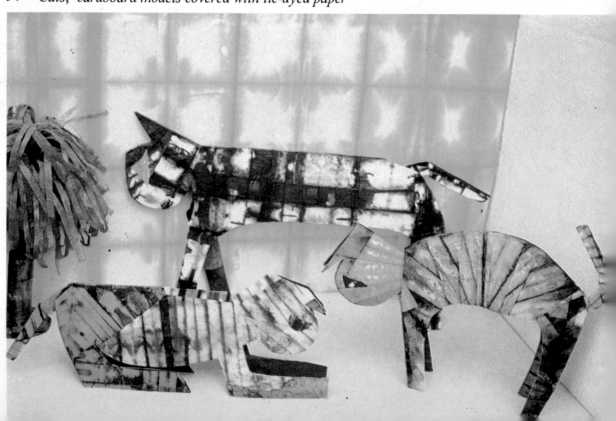

Fold the sample lengthways, then across into a double square WXYZ. Fold the W and X corners down diagonally to the centre to form a double set of right-angled triangles. Add binding or clips.

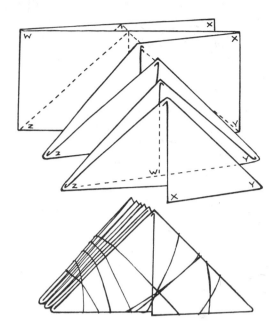

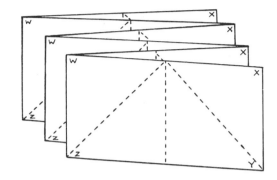

Make the dents on a sample before the first or second dyeing.

Cartridge paper folded lengthways, then zig-zagged across to form a bundle and the corners dented in

Shelf paper folded lengthways and then zig-zagged across to form a bundle. Each corner dented in

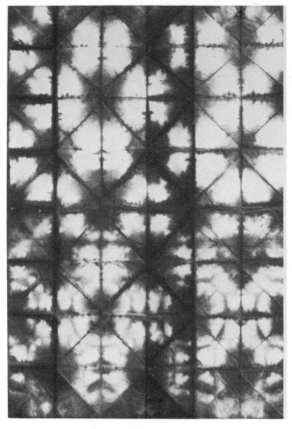

Sides of folds dented in

Folded into a rectangular bundle and both sides dented. M and V folds reversed for second colour

Florist's paper folded in half across, and then as D17. The lower corners dented in and the sample pleated and bound

DYEING

The approach to tie-dyeing paper is rather different from that of tie-dyeing fabric. Fabric needs rinsing, which causes some of the colour picked up to be lost, and has to be laundered, so the dyeing must be permanent. Fabric also soaks up the dye much faster than all but the softest, most absorbent papers. With tie-dyed papers, however, permanence is not so important. It does not need laundering and is only rinsed in special cases, and so it usually retains all the dye it soaks up. The main concern in tie-dyeing paper is to get a good colour and an even penetration of dye.

Whether you use inks or dyes, prepare a strong stock solution of each colour. Store them in tightly corked bottles, labelled with the type and colour. Like this they will keep for many weeks. Shake the bottle before using the dyes. Pour just the amount of dye necessary for the one exercise into the dye vessel. Add water if the colour is too strong, but do not water it down too much or the results will be wishy-washy. Strong colours give the most pleasing results.

The dyed papers will dry paler than they appear when wet. Except on absorbent papers (which in any case are only dip-dyed), a longer dyeing time gives a deeper colour on most papers. When using a new type of paper for the first time, test it to see how it reacts to the dye.

The length of dyeing time for a particular sample is one of the most important factors in tie-dyeing paper. The approximate times given below are for cold dyeing.

Absorbent papers need a short dip in the dye of 5–20 seconds. The dye can also be applied with a brush.

Medium absorbent papers should be immersed in the dye for 30 minutes–1 hour.

Harder, less absorbent papers usually require more than 1 hour. Some will soak up sufficient dye in 2–4 hours; others need longer, even overnight or 24 hours.

Hot dyeing increases the rate of penetration and often produces a deeper colour. This means that the dyeing time for hot dyeing can be reduced to half the time given for cold dyeing. Do not dip soft, absorbent papers in hot dye or they may disintegrate.

The degree to which the dye penetrates a sample has a great influence on the success of the design. The following three points should be taken into consideration.

(*a*) *Size of the sample* Small samples are easier to dye successfully than larger ones, as the colour is spread more evenly over the whole design. It is much more difficult to get an even, well-distributed pattern on a large sample, especially with only one dyeing. Spread the folding out lengthways, dye in sections, or tie-up and dye more than once. (See also pages 91–92.)

(*b*) *Binding* Loose, open binding allows the dye to penetrate to the inner folds. Tight binding, whether in thick bands or over polythene, excludes the dye from that area, so that only the outside layers of the bundle become coloured. (See also pages 36–38.)

(c) *Bulk of the bundle* A thin, spread-out sample presents the dye with large areas of loose paper, which soak up the colour easily. A tightly-folded, thick bundle does not allow the dye to penetrate to the inside, so only the outside edges are coloured. (See page 38).

CHOOSING COLOURS

Choose the strongest, brightest colours available when buying your inks or dyes. You can always tone them down to your taste by mixing or over-dyeing two colours on the sample. A small range of colours can, when mixed together, produce a wide spectrum of secondary colours.

For a limited range of three colours choose:
    deep golden yellow
    bright crimson
    bright blue.
Mixtures:
    yellow + crimson = orange.
    yellow + blue = green.
    blue + crimson = purple.
    yellow + blue + crimson = browns   and greys.

For a range of five or six colours choose in the order below:
    yellow
    crimson
    turquoise blue
    navy or dark brown or black
    purple
    (scarlet)

COLOURING MATTER OTHER THAN DYES

Any liquid that colours paper can be used for tie-dyeing. A few initial experiments can be tried out without incurring any expense. Bunch up or fold some waste paper and dip it in liquid coloured with poster paints, water colours, or similar colouring agents. You will see how easy it is to do. After experimenting for a time it will be worth your while buying some dyes or inks that give more satisfactory results.

SCHOOL POWDER COLOURS

Most schools are provided with powder colours so it would be a simple matter to make a few trial samples, although these paints have a rather limited use. The colour remains on the surface of the paper and the duller, paler colours do not compare favourably with the brilliance and glow of dyes and inks.

Mix the powder colour with water to which has been added enough gum, Polycell or PVA adhesive (approximately one teaspoon to $\frac{1}{4}$ litre or 9 fl oz) to make it adhere to the paper.

Form some small pieces of paper into simple folds. Put a peg on one side or one corner and hold it while dipping the sample in the liquid colour. The colour can be brushed over the lower part of the sample. Drain off the trickles and place on newspaper to dry. Remove the peg and refold the paper. Put the peg on again and colour a different section of the sample with a second colour. Allow the two colours to intermix. Drain, dry and undo.

The powder does not dissolve in the water, so it does not spread out like dyes and inks. Only the parts of the sample that come into direct contact with the liquid pick up the colour. Leave the bundle fairly loose so that the colour can enter or trickle into the gaps and openings of the creases.

BRUSHO COLOURS AND POWDERED INKS

These provide a wide range of brilliant transparent colours that can be mixed together. They are very satisfactory, easy to use and will keep for many weeks stored in air-tight bottles. On most papers Brusho and other inks have a greater degree of penetration than dyes. This is an advantage where large samples, thickly-folded bundles, or less absorbent papers are involved. Brusho is also useful for fragile papers that only need a very quick dip.

Each small carton of Brusho contains enough powder to make a half litre of very strong colour. Mix the powder with cold or warm water. Dye cold. Use Brusho in the same way as dyes for cold dyeing. When using soft, absorbent paper, add a slight thickening of gum or Polycell to the liquid to stop the colour from soaking right through the bundle.

Brusho dyed hot has a much greater and quicker penetration, and should only be used for short dyeings of very bulky bundles, otherwise the resist pattern will be obliterated.

DYES

Nearly all dyes suitable for dyeing cotton can be used for paper.

MAKING STOCK SOLUTIONS

It is convenient to have stock solutions of the colours you will be using ready mixed, stored in bottles. Never put any used dye back into the stock solution. If there is any dye left over, store it separately. In this way your stock solution remains constant and uncontaminated by other colours.

HOUSEHOLD DYES, DYLON MULTIPURPOSE, ETC.

Paste the dye powder from one tin or packet with a little cold water. Add ½ litre (17 fl oz) of boiling water and two teaspoons of salt. Stir.

All liquid dyes: add ½ litre (17 fl oz) of boiling water and two teaspoons of salt to one cap measure of dye. Stir.

Rit and Tintex: Paste contents of package with a little cold water. Add 1 litre (35 fl oz) of boiling water and one tablespoon of salt. Stir.

DIRECT DYES

These give very good, strong colours. There is a slight tendency for them to 'rub' when dry, but this is only a minor drawback and is far outweighed by their positive qualities. All the colours can be mixed together.

Paste one level teaspoon dye powder with a little cold water. Add ½ litre (17 fl oz) of boiling water and two teaspoons of salt. Stir.

BASIC DYES

These give powerful and brilliant colours, but will fade quite easily in strong sunlight. Mix in the same way as the direct dyes.

Most of the dyes mentioned above are improved if, after mixing, they are brought to the boil to ensure that all the dye particles are dissolved, especially when they are to be used for cold dyeing. Cool before putting into glass containers.

REACTIVE DYES

These include Dylon Cold water dyes, Procion M and H, and all reactive dyes produced by other manufacturers. They give excellent results and are made in a wide range of bright colours that can be mixed together.

For fabric dyeing, the working life of reactive dye solutions, once the soda has been added, is only 1–3 hours. After this they will not fix on the fabric, but come away in the wash and rinse waters. For tie-dyeing paper, however, they can be used over several weeks. This is because tie-dyed papers need no rinsing. The left-over dye from fabric dyeing can be saved for tie-dyeing paper.

Where tie-dyed papers may come into contact with food, it is safest to use reactive dyes and rinse the dyed samples. For this purpose mix the dye afresh and immerse the samples in it immediately. Freshly-mixed dye becomes more permanently fixed on the paper, so it will withstand being rinsed better than older dye. The rinsing will make the colour a little paler, but the sample will be less liable to stain any food-stuffs or other objects with which it might come into contact.

STOCK SOLUTION

Dissolve two teaspoons salt and one teaspoon soda (sodium carbonate) crystals in $\frac{1}{2}$ litre (17 fl oz) hot water. Stir until dissolved.

Mix either one small tin Dylon Cold water dye, or one teaspoon Procion M or H, or any other reactive dye with three tablespoons hot water. Add the salt/soda solution to the dye solution and stir.

THE DYEING PROCESS

For all kinds of inks and dyes.

COLD DIP-DYEING FOR ABSORBENT PAPERS

Begin with a small sample, such as a paper napkin. Fold it over several times in any direction. Put a peg on one side or corner. Hold the peg while immersing the opposite side or corner of the sample in the dye for 5–10 seconds. Drain the surplus dye back into the dye bowl (see page 96), and then place the sample on newspaper to drain and dry.

The sample can be rearranged and redipped if required. Leave an area of undyed paper in between the two colours or allow them to intermingle.

Quite often children wish to dye a second or third colour before the first one is dry. For this, pour out small quantities of different colours in shallow bowls, old cups or cartons. If a dyed sample is put into another colour while it is wet, some of the first colour mixes with the second colour on the sample itself and in the dye bowl. After

Paper napkin (left) folded diagonally, pegs added and corners dip-dyed in different colours, and (right) folded diagonally with clip added

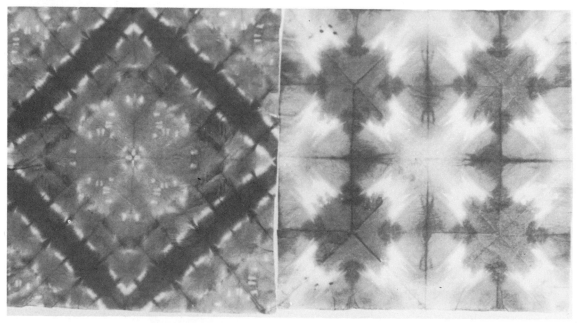

several wet dippings the colours in the bowls become muddy looking, and may have to be thrown away. This is why putting very small amounts of dye in small containers is recommended.

To change the position of the peg without getting dye on the hands is a simple matter.

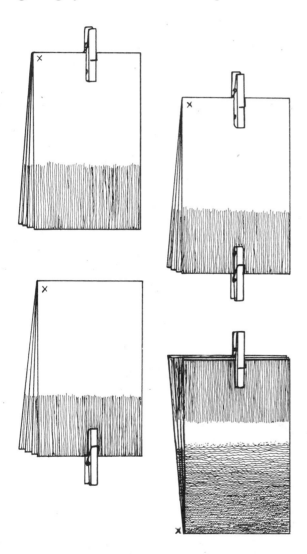

After dipping the sample in the first colour, drain off the surplus dye. Hold the first peg while applying the second one on the wet, dyed area. Remove the first peg to release the undyed parts. Hold the second peg while dipping the undyed parts in the second colour. Drain. Change the pegs again if a third colour is to be used. All four corners can be dipped in various coloured dyes in this way. The finished effect may be just blobs of colour, but adults as well as children will thoroughly enjoy themselves dabbling with the different colours. Afterwards it will be easier to settle down to more organised tie-dyeing. Incidentally, some gloriously colourful abstract designs have unexpectedly been created from these colour dipping experiments.

COLD DYEING FOR MEDIUM ABSORBENT PAPERS

The majority of papers that will be used for tie-dyeing are in this category. They need a far longer dyeing time than the quick dip required by the soft, absorbent papers. The main concern is not how to keep the dye out, but how to get it to penetrate sufficiently so that the pattern is well-dyed and evenly distributed over the whole paper.

Size is an important factor. There is no problem in dyeing a small piece of paper because a major portion of the surface is on the outside of the bundle where the dye can operate fully. It is sensible, therefore, to begin with quite small samples, 10 × 15cm (4″ × 6″), 15 × 20cm (6″ × 8″), or squares of 15cm (6″) or 20cm (8″), and to gradually build up enough experience in handling these successfully before tackling larger ones. Immerse small samples in cold dye for 30 minutes, or until a satisfactory penetration and depth of colour has been achieved.

With larger samples a smaller proportion of the paper's surface is on the outside of the tied-up bundle and exposed to the full action of the dye. There is far more paper inside the bundle than on the outside. As the paper is not immediately absorbent, it takes longer for the dye to penetrate to the inner folds – if it does so at all.

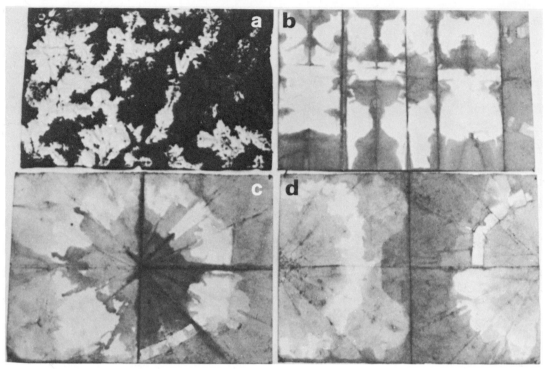

Four small dyed samples: (a) marbling, (b) folded across, then into a bundle (c) folded into quarters, centre and corners dip-dyed, (d) made into an arrow shape, a peg added and both ends dyed different colours

The following suggestions will help you to achieve a good dye penetration on medium absorbent papers.

(*a*) Dye in cold dye for 1–4 hours, or dye in hot dye for approximately half that time.

(*b*) Fold the sample predominantly lengthways, and put bindings and pegs at intervals. Squeeze open the area in between the bindings or pegs into a concertina shape.

(*c*) For a second dyeing, rearrange so that the undyed parts are on the outside of the bundle.

(*d*) Make sparse bindings for the first colour. Reverse the valley and mountain folds and bind before dyeing the second colour.

(*e*) Put pegs on one side only for the first colour. Change the pegs to the opposite side of the bundle for the second colour.

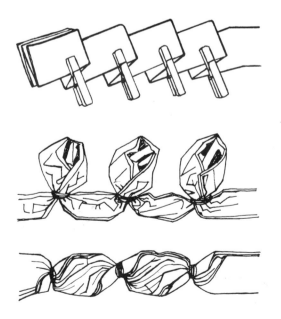

(*f*) Leave some parts free from binding or pegs for the first dyeing. Add extra bindings and pegs for the second dyeing.

(*g*) Soak the tied-up bundle (not 'woolly' paper) in cold water before dyeing.

HINTS FOR DEALING WITH VERY LARGE SAMPLES

All the following suggestions are for a preliminary colouring of the paper. After dyeing, dry and straighten out or iron the samples. Then tie them up in the method chosen and dye for 1 hour or more, depending on the absorbency of the paper.

Make a few simple folds. Use pegs or clips on any samples where binding would squeeze them in too much. Dye in a wide, shallow bowl. Do not move the samples about too much. Swill the dye over and around the samples by tilting the bowl from side to side, or gently pour the dye over them with a spoon.

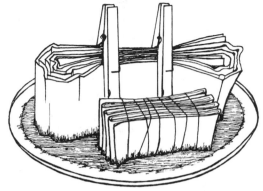

How to dye the edges of the fold (see also page 94)

Two identical tied up samples: (left) this sample dyed DRY; (right) this sample soaked in water for 15 minutes before dyeing

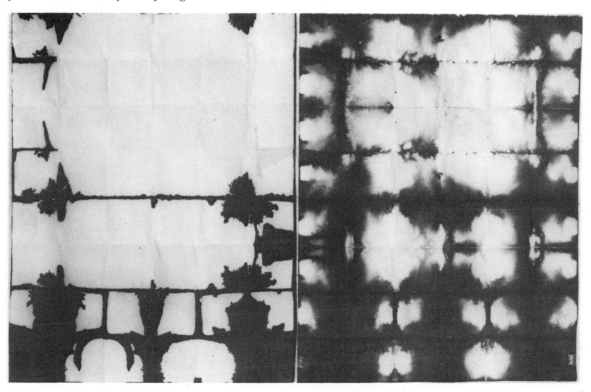

Large sample dyed in sections to produce an all-over pattern

Dip the ends, edges and corners of a single or folded sheet of paper into dyes, not necessarily of the same colour.

Bunch up the paper as for marbling (see page 39), without creasing it too heavily. Put on a loose, sparse binding, just enough to keep it together. Place on top of the dye and let it float, turning it over occasionally. Remove it when enough dye has penetrated the sample.

Fold into four lengthways, wrap round a large tin or bottle, put on a rubber band and stand the base in dye coming about halfway up the sample.

Put a loose crumpled paper inside the toe of a nylon stocking and dip in dye for a short time.

Two large samples showing areas of colour dyed as a preliminary patterning

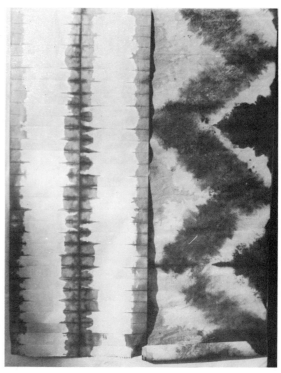

Dye bands of colour on the background before tying up the sample properly. Fold loosely (see diagrams 7–11, page 59) and dye the edges. Repeat, folding the paper in the opposite direction. This will give bands or stripes at right angles to the first ones, forming a rough plaid pattern.

Form the paper into a loose roll or cone. Dye each end a different colour, allowing the excess dye to trickle back over the paper.

Make the sample into a loose twist. Do not bind. Hold each end and gently swing the roll through the dye from left to right and back again, or until sufficient dye has penetrated the sample.

A TWO-TONED EFFECT ON MEDIUM ABSORBENT PAPER

To get a two-toned effect with one dyeing, fold the sample. Add pegs to one side or one end of the bundle. Immerse the entire sample for a short time in shallow dye. Then raise the peg and part of the bundle above the dye, leaving the lower edge immersed for the remaining dyeing time to produce a deeper colour.

When opening up a bundle, if the dye is only on the knife edges of the folds, partially or completely remove the binding, but leave the sample folded. Put a peg in the centre and dip the whole loose bundle or some parts of it in dye for a few seconds. This infuses a paler colour and gives a two-toned design.

ADDING EXTRA COLOUR TO DYED SAMPLES

When a dyed sample appears lifeless or lacking in colour, there are many ways of making it more interesting.

Remove some of the bindings, especially at the ends of the bundle, then dye in a fresh colour. If the binding has been taken off, fold the bundle in half, put a peg on the fold and invert the ends in the dye. This can be done whether the sample is wet or dry.

Treat the centre of the bundle in the same way. Undo the centre bindings, or if already undone, fold the bundle in half, put a peg on the cut edges and dye the loop made in the middle.

To add extra colour to specific areas of a long bundle, make a loop or loops where required, hold in place with pegs or a loose binding and immerse the tips of the loops in dye.

If you can see that the dye has not penetrated well except on the edges, cut the binding quickly and open the sample very carefully while it is still wet. There may be trickles of dye in the valley folds; add extra dye with a spoon or brush and allow it to run along the indentations. Leave the paper open and flat to dry, or fold it, enclosing the runny dye, and press between newspaper. This spreads the dye, giving unusual shapes. Various coloured dyes can be used on the one sample.

Distribute the trickles of dye by smudging with the finger or dabbing with a screwed up knob of paper. Dry samples can also be treated this way.

FLOATING SAMPLES

Occasionally tied-up bundles, especially small ones, float on the surface and will not stay submerged. If this happens, try one of the following remedies.

Hold them down under the dye with a spoon until enough dye has soaked in the paper to 'sink' them.

Cover with a saucer, tin lid, etc., and weight this down with a stone.

Push the samples under the dye, in a small bowl, and cross two spoons over them so that they cannot rise again.

Tie the bundle to the end of a stick, and stand the stick down in the dye.

Turn the samples over at intervals if they persist in floating, so that each side gets its turn in the dye.

APPLYING AND BRUSHING ON EXTRA DYE

Put the ends, corners, or edges of dyed or undyed tied-up samples in a bowl containing a small quantity of dye. Brush the dye over the bundles until a sufficient amount soaks in. Drain off the excess dye at the edge of the bowl, then put the bundles on newspaper to dry. Repeat, using different colours on other parts of the sample.

Hold a previously dyed, wet sample by a peg or clip while brushing dye on various parts, allowing the colours to blend with each other.

Run a brush flooded with a contrasting coloured dye along the edges of the folds of a tied-up bundle after it has been dyed. This treatment can also be given after the bundle has been undone.

Sit the sample on a flat container, such as a saucer, tin lid, or, for very small samples, a spoon. Trickle a small amount of dye into the container until it has seeped up into the edges of the folds for a little distance. When finished, place the sample with the undyed side downwards on newspaper if you want the dye to spread further, or with the dyed side downwards so that it drains on to the newspaper if there is sufficient dye on the sample. This treatment can be given to wet or dry bundles.

HOT DYEING FOR ALL KINDS OF DYES

This gives a stronger colour in a shorter time, and with most papers the dye penetrates further.

Put the required amount of dye in a bowl. Add water if the colour is too strong. Heat the dye to approximately 75°C–85°C (167°F–185°F). Immerse the sample and maintain at this temperature throughout the dyeing period, 15–30 minutes, or longer for tougher papers. Alternatively, put the sample in the dye, heat it to the correct temperature and then take it off the cooker. Leave the sample in the dye until it is cold. Drain and dry. If the paper is strong enough, rearrange and dye a second colour.

RINSING

Usually it is not necessary to rinse tie-dyed papers. Rinsing makes the dyed paper paler, but if you do want to rinse your samples, do it while the bundle is still tied up. This is important, as it prevents the paper from tearing and protects the resist areas, which might get stained by the colour in the rinse water.

Move the bundle about gently in a bowl of water. Do not run water on the sample from the tap because this wears holes in it. If it is a very fragile paper, such as a napkin or soft tissue, place it in a bowl of water, but do not move it about. Tilt the bowl to one side, drain off the stained water and gently renew the water from a jug. Pour the water into one side of the bowl so that it does not agitate the water near the sample. Lift out the sample when it is rinsed. Drain it on newspaper, dry, and unfold.

DRAINING THE SAMPLES

Have plenty of newspaper alongside the dye bowls on which to drain and dry the dyed samples. Where possible, squeeze some of the surplus dye from the samples back into the dye bowl before placing them on newspaper. This can be done in the following ways.

Lift the sample from the dye bowl with a peg, clip, or tongs. Hold the sample against the top edge of the bowl to allow the excess dye to run back into the bowl.

Stand the wet bundle upright in a jam jar, bowl or carton. The dye will drain to the bottom and then can be tipped back into the dye bowl.

Wear rubber gloves or, if they are not available, put a polythene bag over one hand and gently squeeze the bundle over the dye bowl.

Wrap the wet bundle in a piece of polythene, leaving one end open, so that when the bundle is squeezed the dye will flow back into the bowl.

Grip the bundle between two objects, such as spoons, pieces of wood or tin lids, and use them to squeeze out the surplus dye.

Place the bundle on a saucer and press it with a spoon while tilting the saucer sideways.

When a group of children or adults is tie-dyeing, there is soon a heap of dyed samples draining by the dye bowls. Place newspaper on a board or tray. This will hold a large number of samples and is easy to lift up to take away to dry in a warm place afterwards. When the tray is full, place more newspaper on top for a second layer of wet samples.

36 *Examples of tie-dyed biscuit foil wrappings*

37 *Bought paper shoulder bag decorated with cut out design in tie-dyed paper*

38 *Crêpe paper decorations*

39 *Display of tie-dyed greeting cards and bookmarks*

40 *Wall friezes made from small tie-dyed panels*

41 *Decorative panel on a contrasting background*

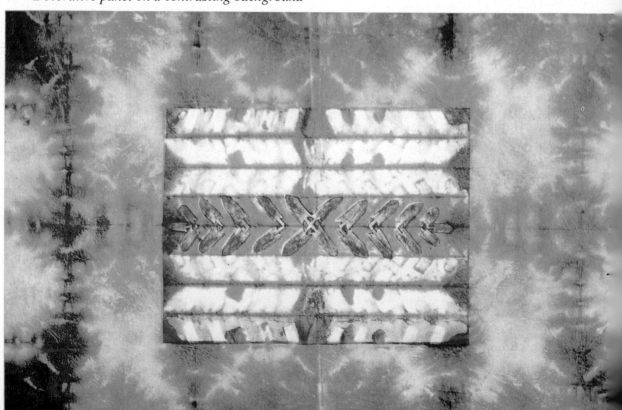

STRAIGHTENING OUT AND IRONING

After drying and undoing, the tie-dyed papers will need flattening and straightening out. Put the paper on a firm, flat surface and press one hand firmly over part of it. Carefully smooth away the creases with the fingers of the other hand and then more firmly with the palms of both hands. Afterwards, put the sample between sheets of newspaper and place it under a flat surface weighted down with heavy objects, or under the carpet.

IRONING

After straightening by hand, many more creases can be removed by ironing.

Iron soft, fragile papers at 'silk' temperature, and medium or tougher ones at 'cotton' temperature. Begin by ironing lightly on the back of the sample and then on the front. Finally, iron both sides again, exerting more pressure. Always use the iron sideways on. If it is pushed in a forward direction, the point can easily dig into the paper, causing a tear or split. Begin at one side or one corner and work across the sample. Try to make a smooth pathway with one hand immediately ahead of the iron. Iron the corners themselves outwards in a diagonal direction towards the point.

If any paper, particularly greaseproof, dries brittle and badly creased, dampen it with a wet cloth, smooth it, place it between sheets of newspaper, pat, and iron it dry. Then remove the newspaper and iron the sample. Take extra care when ironing damp paper because it is weaker, and thus more easily torn, than dry paper. It also tends to stick to the iron. Some of the colour from a damp sample may be transferred to the iron and get deposited on other parts of the paper where it is not wanted. If this begins to happen, cover the damp sample with newspaper. Check before and after ironing that no colour has been deposited on the iron.

An iron should be used only by adults and children under adult supervision.

STORING THE SAMPLES

Keep your tie-dyed paper flat in polythene bags, paper bags or large envelopes. Large sheets should be kept in a folio (two large sheets of cardboard wrapped in brown paper will do), or laid flat in between sheets of newspaper. This prevents extra creases developing. Make very large pieces into a loose roll, cover it with newspaper and tie it to stop it from slipping undone and getting dog-eared and torn at the edges.

Sometimes a tie-dyed paper has some excellent bits of pattern, but the rest lacks interest. Cut off and save the best pieces. Retie and redye the leftover pieces individually.

Save all the tiny waste pieces that are cut off from shapes used in other projects. Store them in polythene bags so that the pieces can be seen and found when they are required for making pictures and models.

The dyed papers should be kept dry. As they have not been rinsed, the colours might run if they get wet.

WEAK SPOTS, HOLES AND TEARS

These need not be disastrous and there is no need for undue disappointment. The damaged pieces can be used for many purposes. After a while you will develop enough know-how in handling the various papers to avoid really bad mishaps. But even with careful treatment there will be times when weak spots, holes and tears appear in your samples. Treat them in the following ways.

TEARS

Place the sample face down on a flat surface and try to fit the torn edges together by straightening and unfurling them with your fingers. When the edges have been coaxed together, stick a patch on the wrong side of the paper without moving the sample. If similar paper is used, the tear will be almost invisible.

HOLES

When cutting out shapes from a tie-dyed sample, the obvious thing to do is to dodge the holes. Where a hole comes in the visible part of a project, superimpose another small shape, in keeping with the design, over it. The accidental hole can be cut into a planned shape as part of the design. Back it with a different coloured paper.

To mend a hole, place the torn part face down on a flat surface covered with newspaper. Coax any stray edges into the centre of the hole, smoothing them very gently with the fingers. A large hole may need some small pins stuck in horizontally around the edges to hold them together.

Then place the iron down on this spot only. Press very firmly without moving the iron. Remove the pins and immediately paste on a patch of the same paper. Now iron the sample in the normal way, back and front. If necessary, the front of the patch can be touched in with dye to match the surrounding paper.

WEAK SPOTS AND SPLITS

Try to cut along these when making articles. Splits usually follow the lines of the folds made in the tying-up. Try cutting open any split and inserting a narrow band of paper in a contrasting colour, making it an integral part of the design. Strips or shapes can be pasted over weak areas and splits, or you can strengthen the samples by pasting a sheet of thin paper on the back.

When smoothing any damaged areas with an iron, keep the point itself away from them; it can easily get caught in tears and holes and make them worse.

ADHESIVES

Almost any gums or glues can be used on tie-dyed paper. Polycell (a wallpaper adhesive) is cheap, easy and quick to mix and will keep for a long time in a screw-top jar. It washes off brushes and hands very easily. Flour-and-water paste and fabric printing gums can be used for backgrounds and very large areas. Always test to see if the adhesive leaves a blotch on the front of the paper. If it does, try one that is drier and stronger, and does not soak through the paper as readily. PVA adhesives are often useful in this respect. One way to avoid blotches is to spread the adhesive sparsely on the background or backing only, then place the top layer over it and press down firmly. Another way is to paste the top layer down only in certain areas where it is possible to hide any blotch made by pasting over it another small shape of thicker paper that will not mark. For instance, the centre of a thin paper flower can be firmly pasted down and then a circle of thicker paper stuck over it to represent stamens. In this case the rest of the flower – the petals – would be left unstuck and loose.

Very absorbent papers are sometimes a problem to stick down without the gum showing through on the front. Try using Ademco, a photographic mounting tissue for fusing two surfaces together. It is sold in various sizes. Place Ademco tissue between the shape and the background, smoothing with a hot iron at 75°C–85°C (167°F–185°F) for 15 seconds or until the fusion has taken place effectively. Iron on both sides. Ademco does not discolour or mark, so it is most convenient for sticking down tissue paper and other semitransparent, fragile or absorbent papers. You might find other bonding tissues that work in a similar way.

Do not put too much wet adhesive on shapes being applied to a tie-dyed background. It makes the paper so soggy that the colour from underneath is picked up and stains the sample. This happens particularly when the top paper is thin or absorbent. It could spoil the character of the design, or it might be an effect to be deliberately aimed at.

PASTING DOWN LARGE AREAS

Some papers stretch, particularly greaseproof, creating crinkles and air pockets when pasted down. Spread a strip of paste about 3–5cm (1¼″ – 2″) wide along the top of the supporting paper and place the top paper carefully along it. Press. Roll the top paper back and paste a further strip. Then smooth the top paper in place, using an iron if possible. Continue working on small sections at a time, making sure that the sides of the two papers are in line.

GROUP WORK

Arrange the tables as close to the sink as possible and so that the maximum number of people can reach the dye bowls easily from all sides. Cover the tables and floor with plenty of newspaper, and have extra newspaper next to the dye bowls on which to drain the samples. The dye bowls should be at fingertip level, if possible, to assure a good view and proper control of the samples. Allow enough room between the dye bowls for people to move from one colour to another without crowding.

Use a separate table, away from the dyes, for tying up the papers. Practise the folding methods with newspaper first, so that they are properly understood before better paper is used. Beginners may prefer to fold and bunch up small pieces of waste paper haphazardly and experimentally to gain experience. These pieces can be used later on for many purposes. After this initial practice, everyone will settle down to tackle more accurate work with a greater feeling of confidence.

Immediately rinse off any dye splashed on the hands. When paper towels are used to dry the hands afterwards, do not waste them; fold or bunch them up, put on a peg and dip *them* in the dye.

When working with young children, use a wide, shallow dye bowl, such as a pie dish. It is less likely to get knocked over than a tall one when a dyed sample is being drained at its side. It also gives more room for dipping samples held by a peg.

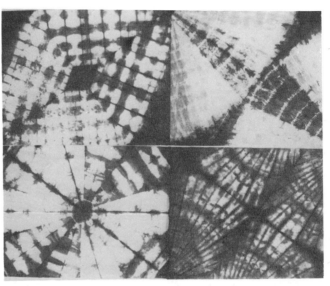

Variations on a theme: four samples of thin resilient paper folded diagonally and then each one treated differently. A fine example of group work

IN SCHOOLS

One adult can manage to keep a watchful eye on approximately ten to twelve pupils. Double that number of children can be accommodated at one session if there is enough room and there are two adults to see that no mishaps occur. It is an advantage to have two adults present when young children are doing the dyeing themselves. If this cannot be arranged, a large class of pupils can tie up the samples at their desks and put them in a bucket containing enough dye to cover all the tied-up bundles. It is more interesting if there are two or three buckets with different coloured dyes so that the children have a choice.

When a particular method is being tried out in a group, get some of the people to improvise changes on the basic theme. This extends their knowledge of each method while they spend time working on only one item.

The name of the individual can be written in pencil or ballpoint pen on the back of the paper.

In a class or group, some people work more quickly than others and have time to spare after completing their samples. To keep them fully occupied, have a supply of odd scraps of paper (waste paper will do) that they can use freely and experimentally without worrying about spoiling them.

Use tie-dyed papers for display in school. Any specimens collected, such as flowers, plants, leaves, shells, stones, etc., look particularly effective placed against a tie-dyed background, even if it is a patchwork of small, odd pieces stuck on newspaper with flour-and-water paste. If items are displayed flat on a shelf or table, cover the surface with tie-dyed paper. Paste attractive panels or cut-outs on window panes or doors, or any glazed areas of the classroom.

After starting tie-dyed paper at school, the children may have many ideas about using it themselves. If they have found it an interesting and stimulating occupation, en-

Collage of marbled and twisted samples to make a background for displaying specimens

courage them to continue with the work at home, pointing out that it can be done in the garden or garage, needs no special equipment, and costs little.

CONSTRUCTING SIMPLE PATTERNS AND DESIGNS

Learning to construct patterns using your own tie-dyed papers is an engrossing occupation. Try to plan designs with both dark and light areas, patterns in which contrasting colours are balanced, and others where harmonious colours blend in with one another.

A rectangle of cartridge paper cut into four pieces and rearranged with the corners together in the centre

Begin with stripes. Cut some narrow strips of light colours and other much wider strips of very bright colours. Alternate them on a darker background in parallel rows and you have a simple stripe pattern. All kinds of variations can be made on this theme; a few examples are given below.

Put two or three narrow strips close together in between two wide strips.

Cut the edges of the stripes into a pattern.

Cut shapes from the middle of the wider stripes and put them in a row on the background to make a stripe of pattern.

Superimpose a thin stripe on a wider one.

Using equally wide dark and light stripes, cut shapes from one side of each and add them to the other stripe (see plate 13).

Vertical stripes crossed over horizontal stripes form a plaid pattern. Put motifs in the spaces and use any of the suggestions given above.

If you make a grid by crossing parallel horizontal and vertical lines, you will see that squares and rectangles have been formed. Add alternate dark squares on a light background and a draught-board design is made.

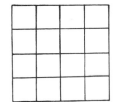
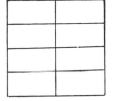

Make one set of parallel lines further apart and you have a rectangular chequered pattern.

Move the square grid around 45° so that you have a diamond design. Cut the diamonds or squares in half diagonally and the result is a triangular pattern.

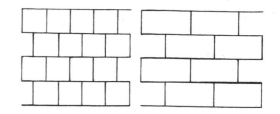

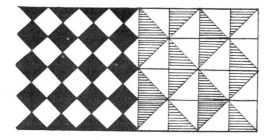

Move alternate rows of squares or rectangles to one side halfway across the shape

above and you have a 'brick' design.

COUNTERCHANGE PATTERNS

A draught board is a counterchange pattern in its simplest form, a balanced arrangement of an equal number of identical dark and light areas. Many fascinating permutations can be worked out on this basis.

The counterchange patterns on plates 13 (top left) and 14 (top) show equal dark and light squares with a triangle cut from one side. Each light triangle is placed in a dark

Counterchange panels: (left) a triangle, diamond, hexagon and octagon arranged within a square; (right) reverse tone effect using pieces cut from first item

square and vice versa. This is a 'Rob Peter to pay Paul' situation. Plate 14 (bottom) shows triangles cut from two sides of each square and placed in the square of the opposite tone. This theme can be greatly varied as long as the pieces cut from the basic shapes are identical and are placed on the basic shapes of the opposite tone or colour. The rule is that nothing must be omitted; whatever is cut from the light shape must be replaced on the dark shape, and vice versa.

If a motif is put in the middle of a pencilled or imaginary square or rectangular grid, the result is a 'spot' pattern. A brick grid can also be used for a spot pattern. Make spot patterns using a diamond and triangular grid, or combine spots with stripes.

A tie-dyed envelope with shapes half cut-out and turned back to complete the design; mounted on a contrasting background

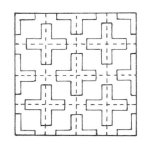

When each corner is cut from a square, the result is a hexagon or an octagon. Round off the corners in a diamond grid and you have what is called an 'ogee' pattern. This lends itself to a design of curving stems, leaves and flowers.

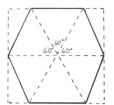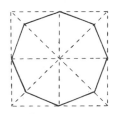

You can go on building and changing in this way. Most designs are based on these elementary principles.

Apart from these continuous or 'all-over' patterns, many intricate and exciting cut-out designs can be created with your tie-dyed papers. Paste these on contrasting backgrounds. Cut out the profile silhouettes of a friend, some well-known person, or birds, animals, plants, etc., and paste them on a tie-dyed paper that shows them up to advantage. Fold a piece of tie-dyed paper into quarters or more. Cut away all kinds of shapes until your sample looks like lace. When cutting a precise or regular pattern, the design can be drawn in pencil on the wrong side to assist the cutting out process.

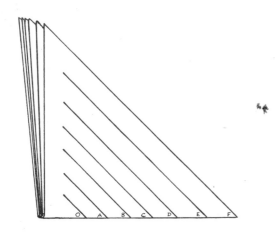

Collage showing the cut out silhouette of a tree

Panel: cut-out and turned-back design mounted on a tie-dyed background

Cut a series of shapes that can be folded and turned back (see the photograph on page 105). Mount on a brightly coloured background and paste various other colours on each turned back piece (opposite).

Create a three-dimensional effect by mounting a cut-out design on a background that itself has some cut-out areas. If this is to be a mobile, leave the cut-out parts on the background as holes. Otherwise, back the cut-out parts with a different coloured paper, creating a design of three colours.

Vertical slits made in sample, some parts turned back and faced with contrasting colours

MAKING COLLAGES AND MURALS

Generally, when a group is working together on a collage or mural, the subject must be decided on deliberately, either because it offers plenty of scope for the imagination or has some bearing on a certain project or lesson. Quite often, though, when a person is working alone and has no special scheme in mind, a certain tie-dyed paper will trigger off an idea because it resembles a tree, running water, a block of flats, or the markings of a flower, bird, animal, etc. In both cases the next step is to sort through the stock of tie-dyed papers, collect any that might possibly be needed for the chosen subject and put them in a polythene bag, where they can be seen at a glance. This reduces the amount of rummaging about necessary to find the sample required.

Collect odd bits of waste paper, small, large, thick, thin, and of different textures. Torn and crumpled pieces are also useful. The white corrugated wrappings from packets of biscuits are invaluable for collages and murals, giving a three-dimensional effect. They also separate into two or three layers, which can be used individually.

Introduce as much variety as possible in expressing the individual features in each collage to create a lively interpretation of the subject. Choose papers and patterns that give the character of the various component parts. For instance, leave the creases in the tie-dyed papers to give the rugged appearance of craggy rocks or the rough bark of trees.

Collage, 'Doorways'

Both light- and dark-toned papers will be needed to give contrast to the composition. Marbled tissue paper is very expressive for areas of sky and clouds or water.

Having chosen a subject and made a wide collection of tie-dyed papers, the next step is to decide whether to select a background first or to complete the separate parts, which can then be assembled on a background that shows them to advantage. In the latter case the background itself can be made of several papers pieced together.

Perhaps a gradation of tone can be arranged so that light objects are placed in front of a darker part of the background and vice versa.

Usually a design is more satisfactory if an object is brighter in colour or more definite in tone than the background on which it is placed.

When a landscape is being depicted the background is part of the scene, so objects and background merge and have to be considered in conjunction with one another.

The individual shapes in the composition can be treated in several ways. If the chosen tie-dyed paper is strong and large enough, the entire shape can be cut from the one piece and pasted directly on the background.

When several kinds of paper are required for one figure or object in the design, first cut out a paper pattern of the entire shape in firm paper (magazine, typing, brown paper, etc.). Then assemble and paste down all the tie-dyed paper sections that make up the whole object. Very small bits of tie-dyed paper can be cut out and stuck on the paper pattern like a mosaic. Another method is to paste odd pieces of tie-dyed paper haphazardly on a backing paper and cut the required figure from it. Very unusual and unexpected effects are produced in this way. On a cut-out pattern of the shape, individual units can be arranged to represent the nature of the object itself, such as feather shapes for a bird, or scales for a fish. If they are pasted down in layers on the background at one end only, leaving part of them unattached, a very rich and lively effect is produced.

When the different features or shapes are complete, shuffle them about on the background until a satisfactory arrangement is achieved. Hold them lightly in place on the background with a fine pin. Before doing this, test to see whether the hole left in the sample by the pin is permanent or can be smoothed down afterwards with the thumb nail to make it invisible. If the paper is spoiled by the pin-hole, put some clean stones or small weighty objects on the loose shapes to keep them stationary until they can be pasted down. A slight margin can be left in odd places on the shapes for putting in the pins, and then cut away just before the shapes are stuck down.

Paste down the underneath layers first. This means temporarily removing the top layers or rolling them back bit by bit while the sticking is done. Next paste down the middle sections and finally the top pieces.

Sometimes when a collage is completed, the background or part of it appears too dominant for the shapes in front. In such cases brush a very pale wash of the dye used in the background paper, or a neutral colour, over the area. Dry it quickly so that the pattern does not run. The original pattern shows through the pale wash although it is toned down considerably.

You will find that textures rather than definite geometric patterns are generally more suitable for backgrounds. Make the nearer objects of clear-cut patterns.

Some features in the designs are greatly enhanced if they are padded out to give a raised, sculptural look. The padding (screwed-up paper) can be stuck to the back of the shape itself or to the background and then have the shape pasted over it. Areas of screwed, pleated or bunched-up paper can be used as part of the design in the collage. Fringes, scallops and points can also be incorporated, leaving some parts free. Try covering small cardboard boxes with tie-dyed papers and using them as component parts of the design.

Newspapers on which samples have been drained and dried after dyeing often make gay and colourful backgrounds with their blurred mixture of indefinite blotches. Strengthen them by pasting two or three thicknesses of newspaper at the back. Reinforce the edges with a gummed paper strip or by turning them back and pasting them down.

Cut-out patterns superimposed on other cut-out patterns and placed on a background that also has cut-away areas provide interesting 'see-through' and three-dimensional impressions.

Exploit the possibility of illuminating semi-transparent papers, such as tissue, by placing them over different brightly coloured sections or patches. Quite startling changes are made in a design when the colours of the papers underneath glow through. In a collage or mural combine the use of double tissue paper that shows only the original dyed pattern with areas where single tissue paper is placed over sections of very bright colours that change the character of that pattern.

'Fir trees and lake' This scene was triggered off by finding two pieces of tie-dyed typing paper, one looking like a pine tree and the other resembling water. The composition is made entirely from rectangular and triangular shapes of different sizes, colours and patterns, assembled to form a landscape. It is quite a challenge to make figures or scenes from simple geometrical shapes. (See plate 19.)

Semi-transparent paper: one half superimposed over a white background, the other half over a dark background

PAPER WEAVING

To make the warp, cut equal lengths of tie-dyed greaseproof or similar paper into strips approximately 3–4cm (1¼″–1½″) wide. Fold each strip into three lengthways and paste closed. Arrange the strips in parallel lines on newspaper and pin down at the top and bottom. You can make the warp of identical strands or dissimilar strands, varying, for example, in colours and widths.

For the weft, cut strips of other tie-dyed papers a little longer than the width of the warp. They can be of various textures, widths, thicknesses, colours, twisted round string, several narrow strands bunched together, or plaited, etc. These can be arranged to form a design. Weave in and out of the warp, allowing a little of the weft to project on either side. Paste down or pin to the background. If pins are used, the piece of weaving will need to be pasted on a backing to hold it together when it is taken off the newspaper.

Dye some string or thread for the warp and attach it to a cardboard backing. Use any of the suggested ways of making the weft.

The pieces of weaving can be made into mats, plant pot covers, dolls' clothes, fancy hats, etc.

The narrow, pasted strips used for the warp are suitable for plaiting, braiding and simple basket work experiments.

Paper weaving: table mat

POSTERS

Very striking posters can be made with tie-dyed papers.

Cut out individual letters from tie-dyed papers. They can be from the same piece of paper, or from papers in differing patterns and colours. The most important words should be of the darkest, lightest or brightest paper. Paste them on a contrasting tie-dyed background.

Use some letters cut in plain paper on a tie-dyed background, or vice versa.

Incorporate motifs, panels of decoration, or small collages in the general design.

Cut away some of the letters from the background and put a brightly coloured mount at the back.

42   'Circus act'

43   'Custard pie versus bucket of water'

ORIGAMI

Tie-dyed papers add another dimension to origami projects. Suitable papers are hand-made, greaseproof, tissue, typing, shelf, cartridge, and florist's papers, and most flexible but firm papers.

The type of paper should be geared to the size of the chosen project. For instance, use tissue paper for small figures, and cartridge or hand-made paper for larger ones. Tissue and fine papers can be used double. Where the animals, birds or figures are grouped together to form a composition, a little reinforcement of stiff card can be inserted inside the models to enable them to stand.

It is possible to use paper that has already been tie-dyed. Tissue paper should be dyed before it is folded into models. With other papers you can make the model of undyed paper, pleat it, add string bindings or pegs, and dye it. When dyeing a second colour, reverse the mountain and valley folds. The two ends of the model can be dyed different colours. Where the first colour is dark and only the edges of the folds are dyed, undo the binding but leave the folds in place. Dip the loose sample in the dye. This gives a unifying and interesting effect. After dyeing the folded model, dry and iron. If this does not remove a sufficient number of the creases, unfold the model, iron the paper flat and then refold it into its former shape.

Bull, origami model in greaseproof paper

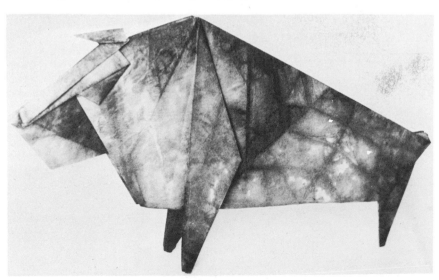

Rabbit family, origami models in tissue paper

Ducks, origami models; two larger ducks in greaseproof paper

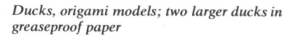

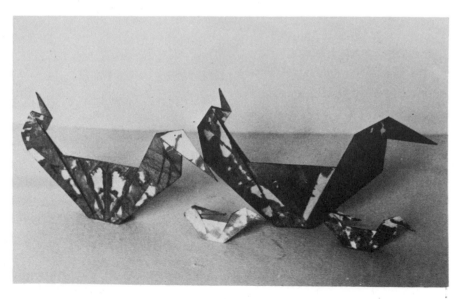

MOBILES

Tie-dyed papers are admirable for making mobiles. They are gay in colour, design and texture. When made of semi-transparent papers, such as tissue, greaseproof, hand-made, etc., the light shining through gives a glow and brilliancy to the colours. When paper is being used double, Ademco or a similar tissue is effective in fusing the pieces together invisibly.

A pattern can be cut out in thicker paper, such as typing paper, and pasted on a semi-transparent tie-dyed backing paper.

Cut out interesting or amusing shapes in brightly coloured thicker paper and place them where the light shines on them, not through them.

Mobiles: butterflies in various papers

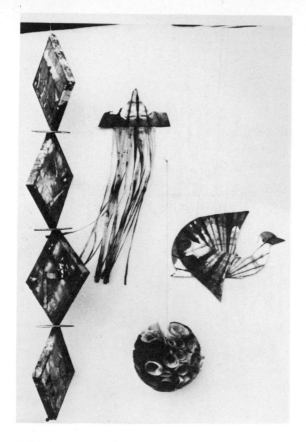

Make shapes and attach loose streamers, hanging flowers, fringes, etc.

Use origami models made of semi-transparent paper as mobiles.

Create three-dimensional models and figures, cover with tie-dyed paper, and suspend them from fine thread or reel wire attached to a frame.

Mobiles

DOLLS

Some really smart outfits for dolls can be fashioned from tie-dyed papers. Cut out the shapes for each part of the costume and stick or sew them together. They can be put together on a thin fabric undergarment.

Making your own paper dolls is a lot of fun. To make a baby doll, form some soft tissues into a firm ball and cover it with a pink paper table napkin. Cut a circle of tie-dyed paper 35cm (14″) in diameter and one 45cm (18″) in diameter. Fold each circle in half; use the smaller one for a skirt and the longer one for a shawl.

simple shapes. Arrange them around the dolls and attach with staples, rubber bands, string, or a strong adhesive.

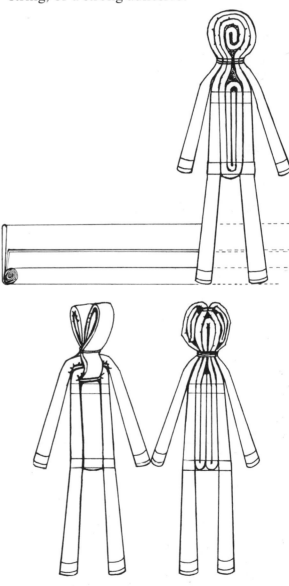

Here is another way to make paper dolls. Roll some sheets of newspaper, 60 × 75cm (24″ × 30″), into firm, hard tubes. Paste down the loose edges and strengthen each end with sticky tape if necessary. Assemble as shown, fasten together with sticky tape, rubber bands or string. Pad out the face and cover with soft, flesh-coloured paper. Paint on the face or cut out shapes for features and stick them on. Add fringed paper for hair. Create gay striking clothes, cut in

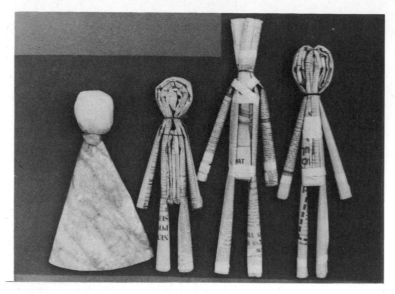

How to make paper dolls. The three on the right are made from newspaper

Cut out cardboard figures and make flat garments in tie-dyed paper to hook on them or to fit round them with strings to tie.

All cardboard or plastic carton models of birds, animals, and people are effective covered with tie-dyed paper. Cardboard outline models that fold over in half can be covered with tie-dyed paper.

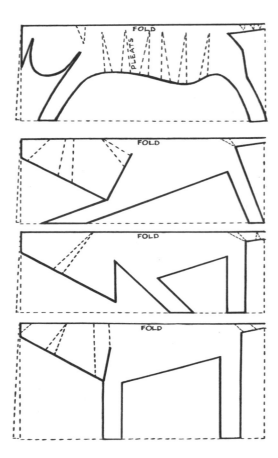

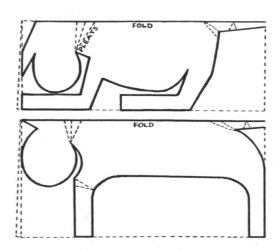

SIMPLE HAND PUPPETS

Dye some white, coloured or brown paper bags. Mould, cut, fold or pad out to create the semblance of a face, whether human, animal, bird or fish. Add separate features where necessary. Attach the prepared bag puppet to the wrist with a rubber band. Alternatively, design a cover-up for the forearm and hand in the form of a skirt, cape, dress, or a body or part of a body, such as wings. Attach the cover-up to the open end of the bag, allowing enough space to put in the hand that works the puppet.

Some origami models made in tie-dyed paper on a fairly large scale can be adapted as hand or glove puppets. Make puppets from small cardboard boxes covered with tie-dyed paper. Full-length puppets can also be made like this. Cover any of the puppets you make with tie-dyed paper or use it for making their costumes.

Jumping Jenny, puppet made from paper bags

MASKS

Large tie-dyed paper bags make good simple masks. Stick on any extra pieces to represent the features and cut the necessary holes. The bags will have to be big enough to pull over the head of the wearer easily.

Flat masks can be attached to a brown paper band that fits round the head like a crown, or have loops of string at the side to fit over the ears. Put some tucks on the outside of the masks, especially under the chin, so that they fit snugly round the face. Some parts of the mask can be made to move – a tongue coming out of the mouth and ears wagging, eyes rolling and hair rising! Sounds grotesque, but it always causes amusement!

For more permanent masks make a framework of strong brown paper or cardboard. Cereal boxes are excellent for this purpose; they are light in weight and, if turned upside down, the bottom of the box can be left intact so that it rests in place on top of the head. Cut out the overall shape. If a box is used, cut down the centre of one of the wider sides to form two flaps that will almost meet at the back of the head. Tie these together with a piece of string to hold the mask in place. Cover with tie-dyed paper. Cut out eyes, nose and mouth. Aim at inventing an exaggerated, fanciful or preposterous image of a face – a complete disguise. This is the whole purpose of a mask, so let your imagination run riot. Incorporate all manner of oddments, dyed matchsticks, matchboxes and cartons, fringed paper and paper flowers, dyed rope for hair, beards and animal fur.

Mask, tie-dyed paper pasted on a cereal box

Mask

FANCY DRESSES

With a little ingenuity some delightful costumes for school plays, pageants and fancy dress parties, and all kinds of accessories can be made from tie-dyed paper. Crêpe, tissue, greaseproof, hand-made, shelf and florist's papers would seem to be the most suitable, as they come in larger sheets. Smaller pieces can be used like patchwork if mounted on a larger sheet or fabric backing. Most complete outfits will require a backing of some kind on which to fix and paste, pin, staple or sew the dyed paper into shape. A few of the possibilities for this are strong brown paper, double or treble newspaper pasted together, Vilene, net, tarlatan, old sheeting, butter muslin and cheesecloth.

A flat seam can be made by pasting the two edges together so that they just meet on a strip of strong paper.

When sewing the shapes on the foundation, make the stitches at least 1 – 2cm ($\frac{3}{8}''$ – $\frac{3}{4}''$) long, or the paper will break away from them as the wearer moves about. A good way is to make a row of tacking stitches from right to left through the paper and the foundation, and then fill in the gaps with stitches, sewing in the opposite direction in the same needle holes. Use the largest possible stitch if the seams are made on the sewing machine.

Make the dresses to slip over the head easily, to step into, or to wrap around and fasten on the wearer. To fasten them, use string ties, tapes or safety pins. The latter can be disguised and covered with imitation paper buttons, buckles, bows or flowers.

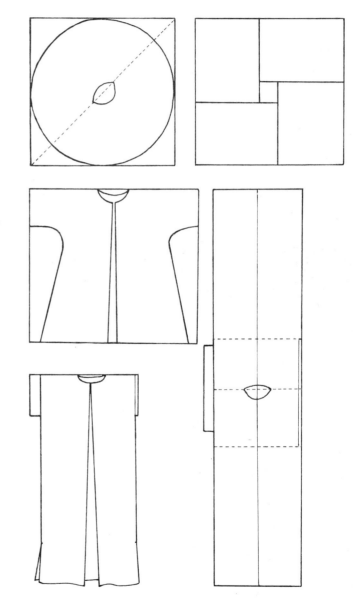

Make square or circular ponchos and tunics. You can add a variety of sleeves to the tunics if you wish.

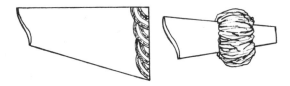

Dresses and skirts are pretty made with layers of frills in crêpe or tissue paper. Decorate the edges by cutting fringes, scallops or a lace pattern. When dipping crêpe paper for costumes, use pegs for holding the bundles, as they do not create 'waists' like heavy binding. Other ideas are listed below.

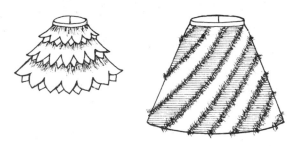

A patchwork skirt or one formed of layers of petals, like a turned down flower head.

Rows of paper feathers on sleeves to imitate a bird's wings.

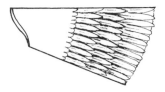

An all-over cut-out pattern in crêpe paper to look like lace. Mount this over a coloured background.

Make paper capes and shawls, gauntlets on gloves, crêpe paper high boots.

Gay tie-dyed paper aprons, decorated lavishly with pasted-on flowers, leaves, hearts, etc.

Make large separate paper feathers. Mount tie-dyed paper on both sides of a thin card. Cut into a feather shape, and then cut both sides into fine fringes.

Keep all the garments simple in shape so that when they are made up they are easy to iron.

HATS

You will love making tie-dyed paper hats – pretty, frivolous, comic ones, copies of historical head-dresses for plays; the possibilities are endless. All kinds of paper can be used. Choose the types most suitable for each particular model. Strengthen the hat with a band of strong brown paper that fits round the head. It can also be used as a foundation on which to mould the hat itself, or for attaching any free-hanging items, such as flowers, leaves, bows, streamers, birds, butterflies, ribbons, frills, or feathers.

Hat made from a large circle of shelf paper, pleated into a cone shape, slits edged with contrasting colour

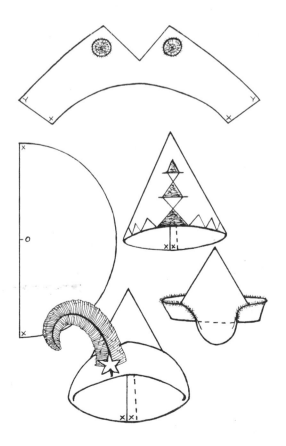

When the paper is strong enough, a rough shape of the hat can be cut out before dyeing. The tie-dyed design can then be arranged in the most appropriate positions. Dye some extra paper in case repairs need to be done afterwards.

Tie-dye some large paper bags that will fit on the head (see photographs on pages 124–125). Pleat and mould them to form head-dresses. If there is printing on the bag, add some form of applied decoration to hide it, or turn the bag inside out before dyeing to make it the wrong side of the sample.

Paper-bag hat

Innumerable styles of hats are easily made from tie-dyed papers approximately 35–50cm (14″–20″) square, folded as shown in the diagrams on this page.

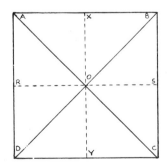

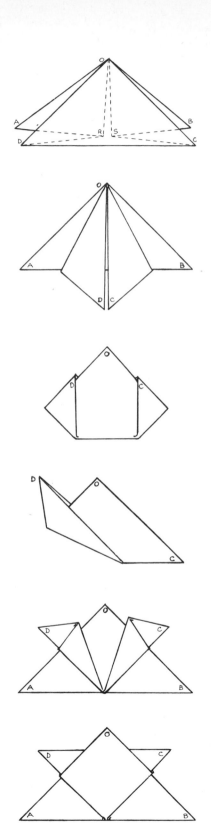

Clown's hat

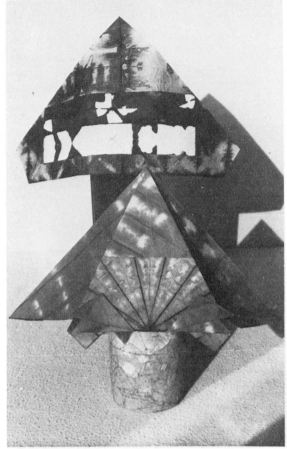

Made from squares of paper, as diagrams

Dignitary's hat

Made from a square of paper, as diagrams

Soft, strong doubled tissue folded in half for bonnet

Made from a square of paper, as diagrams

Tam-O'-Shanter

Crown, cardboard covered with tie-dyed paper

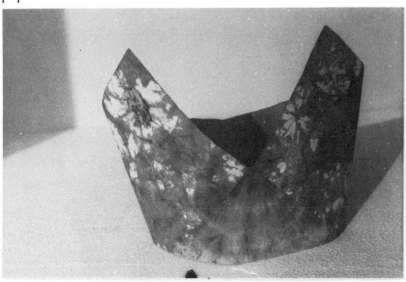

PAPER FLOWERS

Many of us have tried our hand at making paper flowers at one time or another. Why not tie-dye your paper for these the next time? Your special favourites will then take on a very special look.

Begin with simple-to-make flowers in tissue and crêpe paper. Reel wire and lengths of thicker wire for stems can be bought at florists' shops. Look for and save any odd bits of paper that might be useful for petals and leaves. Tie-dye them ready for use. Apart from tissue and crêpe paper you will find greaseproof paper, oven parchment, florist's white paper, fine hand-made paper, and even napkins and doilies can all be turned into pretty paper flowers.

Cut out and dye the amount of paper required for one flower, or dye the various parts of each flower separately. A whole sheet of tissue paper can be tie-dyed and then the most appropriate parts chosen. For instance, the darker parts can be used for the outside of the flower and the paler parts for the inside. One flower can be made up of several colours, or more than one type of paper. Cover the stems with any soft paper that is available; it does not necessarily have to be green. After cutting out the flowers, try brushing a different coloured dye on the tips and outside edges of the petals or dip the centre into a darker dye.

Floral decorations

Three popular ways of constructing paper flowers are illustrated in the diagrams below. With a little ingenuity other kinds can be created.

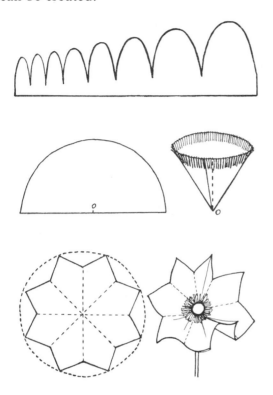

Here are some other suggestions.

Cover real twigs with tie-dyed paper, poster paint or metal paint. Add tie-dyed paper leaves and flowers, singly or in bunches.

Put a group of real twigs, covered or painted, in a plant pot. Put leaves, buds, flowers, birds, butterflies, etc. on this 'shrub'. Put a tie-dyed paper cover round the pot.

Cut a large circle in strong paper and cut away the centre area. Cover with a rich, lush quantity of leaves and flowers made of tie-dyed paper, like a garland. Add bows and paper ribbons. Hang it on the wall or use it as a centrepiece on the table for a party or a special occasion. Make a garland from a circle of rope or wire.

Cover string or fine rope with tie-dyed paper. Insert leaves and flowers at intervals to make a creeper or a climbing plant. This will need a framework or a branch to give it support. The rope itself can be tie-dyed as a stem for attaching flowers and leaves.

Make a long, narrow fringe of crêpe paper. Stick the top to a length of cardboard or wood. At intervals on the fringes attach gaily coloured, rather small flowers and

Fringed paper mobile or wall decoration

leaves. Several of these can be placed along walls or in suitable places. They can be free-hanging so that the air currents set the fringes in motion.

Incorporate dyed matchsticks, beads or other oddments in your flowers.

Pot plant with woven plant pot cover

MAKING THINGS

When you have tie-dyed your papers, it would be a pity not to make full use of them. Here are some ideas for things to do with your papers.

Make Christmas and greetings cards, calendars and bookmarks, matching tray cloths, napkins and doilies, and kites and banners.

Cover an old lampshade. A simple shape is easiest. Stick cut-out motifs on a lampshade.

Stick motifs or other decorations on bought, coloured paper shopping bags.

Stick cut-out decorations on notepaper. Fold the notepaper into quarters to make notelets and party invitations.

Cover books and folios.

Dye a number of panels to paste on the wall at the side of your bed, or in another conspicuous part of your room.

Create a stained glass effect by cutting out shapes of birds, flowers, or fish in semi-transparent paper (greaseproof, hand-made and tissue paper, for example) and sticking them on your window.

Make covers for plant pots for house plants.

Tie-dyed doilies and paper napkins

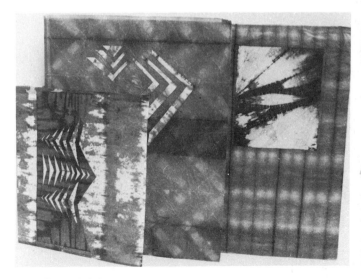

Book and folio covers

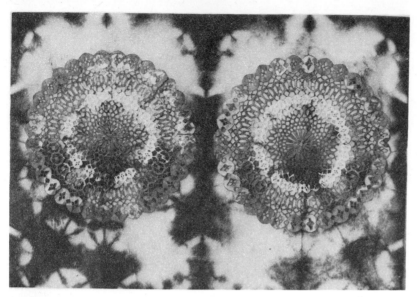

Table mat: tissue paper and doilies

Decorative wall panel

Tissue paper decoration

STREAMERS

Dyed strips of crêpe paper with the edges fringed, pointed or scalloped make colourful streamers, twisted and draped across a room.

Collect from your greengrocer some small tissue paper squares used for wrapping fruit and tomatoes. After tie-dyeing, arrange them on a background for a mural, table decoration, etc.

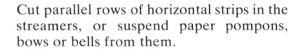

Crêpe paper decorations

Cut parallel rows of horizontal strips in the streamers, or suspend paper pompons, bows or bells from them.

To make pompons, cut a number of circles in tissue paper. Fold them into quarters, roll into a cone, thread on cotton at the centre and tie.

Make Chinese lanterns or crackers to hang on rope.

Cut out a pattern along a narrow length of paper and mount it on a transparent backing.

Tie-dye paper chains and friezes.

OTHER DECORATIONS

Tie-dye paper tablecloths and use them as a base or a background on which to assemble paper flowers, birds, animals, butterflies, and all kinds of cut decorations and models. Use this as the centrepiece for a table display or exhibition, or put on the wall as a hanging.

Make crackers with your tie-dyed papers. Cover bundles of sweets or presents with tie-dyed paper for the party table.

Cut out and cover flower or animal shapes for table decorations.

Face composed of geometrical shapes—rectangles and triangles

A sweet bag for parties. Tie-dye an ordinary white paper bag and add flowers, etc.

Various trees for a model stage

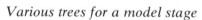

GAMES FOR CHILDREN

Make some tie-dyed animals and birds. Paste them on strong paper, fine card or old greetings cards. Cut each into four sections and mix up the pieces. The children have to sort out the different parts and complete the figure. Extend this idea and make all the sections interchangeable. See who can make the most absurd combination of parts.

Cut out and mount geometrical shapes on fine card. Piece the various shapes together to form a figure or object.

Make a model theatre from a cardboard box and cover it in tie-dyed paper. Cut out tie-dyed paper figures and mount them on card, or make tie-dyed paper puppets.

Paper hats competition. Have lots of tie-dyed paper available, as well as boxes, cardboard, and other oddments, and pins, string and adhesives. Allow children 30 minutes for hat making, and then have a parade to find the best hat.

A model-making session can be run in the same way.

Give instructions for simple origami models and pick out the best example.

Give six old envelopes to each person. See who can produce the most attractive and original object from them. If there is time, they can do the dyeing themselves, but if not, the envelopes can be dyed beforehand.

In a combined effort, compose a limerick, and select the best tie-dyed paper illustration of it. (See plate 45.) It was created to illustrate the following limerick.

"You can hear from afar Mr Tra-la-la-lay,
He was brought up on music from youth, so they say.
With heels tapping, head waving and baton in hand,
You'd think he was conducting a real live band,
And he never stops singing throughout the whole day.'

Similarly, a well-known real or imaginary character can be chosen and an award made for the best interpretation in the form of a portrait or three-dimensional model.

SUPPLIERS

The majority of items required for tie-dyeing paper are easily obtained from large stores or the appropriate shops in your locality. Colleges and schools are able to order what they need from their central supplies department.

Dylon International Ltd
Worsley Bridge Road
Lower Sydenham
London SE26 5HD

Dylon multipurpose and cold water dyes can be bought from shops and stores in small tins and 30g tins. Liquid dyes are also available. 1lb or 500g tins can be obtained from the address above.

Skilbeck Bros Ltd
Bagnall House
55–57 Glengall Road
London SE15 6NQ

Supply Solamine (direct) dyes in 1lb or 500g tins, basic dyes in 4oz tins, and Procion dyes in kilo tins.

Candle Makers Supplies
4 Beaconsfield Terrace
London W14 0PP

Supply basic, direct, and Procion dyes in 1oz and 4oz cartons, and Sennelier (basic) dyes in tubes. They also stock hand-made papers.

J. B. Duckett Company Ltd
74 Broadfield Road
Sheffield S8 0XL

Supply Brusho in packs of 24 cartons

T. N. Lawrence & Son Ltd
2–4 Bleeding Heart Yard
Greville Street
London EC1N 8SL

Supply hand-made and special papers

Paperchase
216 Tottenham Court Road
London W1

and

167 Fulham Road
London SW3

Supply a varied selection of papers, including some hand-made, and have a mail order service (inquire about their terms).

The *Studio Vista Guide to Craft Suppliers* is a useful reference book.